Published by
Grandreams Limited
435-437 Edgware Road, Little Venice,
London, W2 1TH.

Printed in Hong Kong.

THE BIG BOOK OF

MAGIC

INTRODUCTION
FROM ALI BONGO

Welcome to the wonderful world of magic. I'll bet most people have wished at some time that they could say a few magic words or wave a wand to make marvellous things happen. Unfortunately, that kind of magic is not really possible, but this book will teach you some amazing tricks that you can use to entertain your friends. All you need are a few simple items found around the house, plus a little preparation and a certain amount of practise and rehearsal, and you will be able to put on a super magic show.

Also included in the pages that follow are some more complicated tricks that will require a little construction work, but the effort will be worthwhile when you see the effect on your audience. Building your own magical apparatus can be just as much fun as performing with it.

One very important thing to remember is that magic is part of the art of entertainment, which means helping people to enjoy themselves. It would not be a good idea to stand up in front of your friends and act as if you were much cleverer than any of them, because that would only make everyone want to catch you out – and that's no fun at all! It's far better to be pleasant and amusing, because if an audience likes you they will like your tricks too.

If this is your first book of magic, I hope you will enjoy learning about this fascinating occupation, which is a very old one, and has been going on from the beginning of time. The first cave-man who struck two flint-stones together and created fire was a fantastic magician in the eyes of his companions. The first recorded magician in history is known to have performed for the Pharaohs of Egypt, and there were priests in the ancient Greek temples who used magic tricks to make their followers believe that they possessed mystical powers.

Apart from being a very old profession, magic is a wonderful hobby. All round the world people get together in magic clubs to show each other their latest tricks, and exchange ideas. You will discover that being a magician makes you a member of one of the friendliest groups of people in the world. Have fun, and welcome to the club!

Ali Bongo

Practise makes perfect

Most magicians say that practise is the most important thing, but really before that you must PLAN your tricks very carefully, and THEN practise thoroughly so that you know them inside out. Think about every move you make, and see if you can improve it in any way. Try rehearsing in front of a mirror, to see yourself from the spectators viewpoint.

Arrange the props on your table so that you can pick things up in the right order, and cannot get into a muddle. Make a drawing to show the position of the props so that you can arrange them the same way every time. This helps to give you confidence, so that you don't have to stop to think what comes next.

Your programme

Every magic show should have a definite order, and the most important parts are the start and the finish. Your first trick should be quite short, simple to follow, but strong in effect so that you get applause. Then you can do some longer, more complicated tricks for the middle part, making them as varied as possible. The last trick should be fairly spectacular to make sure it is the one that gets most applause. It must be quite clear to everyone that it is your "Big Finish".

What to wear

It is not really important what you wear when you are performing a few tricks at home, or for friends at a party, although it is always useful to wear a jacket with its handy pockets. However, when you are doing a show on a stage, boys should always dress as smartly as possible in a suit and tie, and girls in a nice neat dress, preferably in plain colours. The reason is that your clothes form a background to the tricks, so your colourful props will show up better against a plain dress or suit.

Of course, you may prefer to be more adventurous, and dress up in fancy costume such as Chinese, or Indian, or as a Wizard. But the same advice about plain colours and fabrics still applies, and you should avoid using contrasting patterns that could confuse the eyes of your audience. Also, if you decide to do a performance in a character costume, you must choose your tricks to fit in with the style of the costume, and decorate your apparatus appropriately.

Your magic table

Make sure you use a good strong table that won't collapse in the middle of your performance. It would probably get a laugh, but not the kind you want! Try to avoid your table looking cluttered up with too many props. It's a good idea to have a box on the table and keep all your props hidden in it

JLES OF MAGIC

until you need them, and a waste-paper basket on the floor, to take all the items as you finish with them.

Stage setting

A plain, darkish background is usually best for magic, and always make sure you have plenty of light so that people at the back of the room or hall can see clearly. For a large place, use a microphone if one is available. Remember, magic is no good at all if it cannot be seen and heard.

Music

Even if you do a talking act, it is quite a good idea to have a little SOFT music playing in the background. The more showy and spectacular tricks, where there is lots of action, are usually better performed silently to carefully selected music. This can be recorded, but it is really far nicer to have live musicians, because then it is much easier to change the music to suit each trick, and they can give you a big chord at the end to help build up the applause.

What to say

Always try to be natural when you are planning what to say. Avoid complicated words that might tie your tongue in knots, and long-winded stories or explanations that hold up the action. After all, magic is a VISUAL entertainment and your audience wants to SEE something happen.

Applause

Some words of advice on a very important subject. If you perform well, your audience will always WANT to applaud, so you must help them to do so by letting them know the right moment. The best way to do this is to have a clear-cut finish to each trick, STOP, then LOOK at your audience expectantly, and WAIT until they applaud. Be sure to acknowledge the applause with a grateful smile.

Keeping your secrets

If someone asks you how your tricks are done, just tell them that magic wouldn't be any fun if everyone knew all the secrets – then quickly distract them by showing another trick. Try not to repeat your tricks in front of the same audience, because every time they see it, it makes it easier for them to work out how it's done.

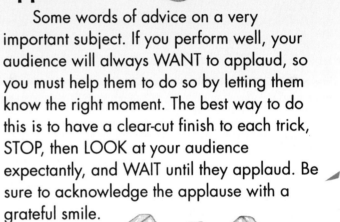

HAPPY MAGIC MAKING!

CONTENTS

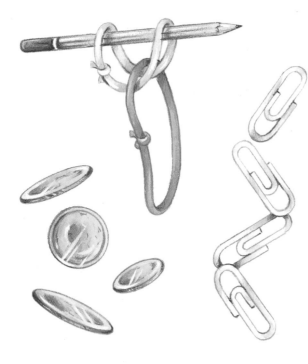

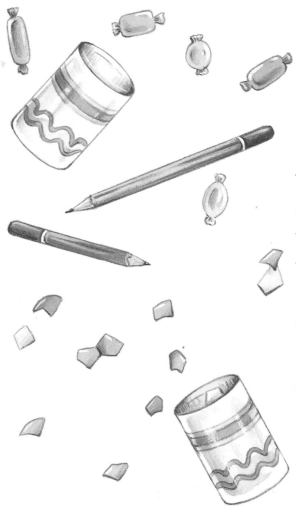

THE WIZ

In this trick your audience sees a sheet of plain dark-coloured paper on the table. On it are placed a small glass or plastic tumbler, upside down, together with a miniature wizard's hat. You ask someone to lend you a small coin, which is placed on the centre of the paper.

SHAPE- FOR MAKING WIZARD'S HAT

PAPER DISK TO GLUE ON

Then you lift up the wizard's hat, drop it over the glass, pick up both together, and place them over the coin. Now you say the magic words, "Hey Presto, make the money go!", then lift up the hat by itself. Your friends will be able to see through the clear sides of the glass that the coin has completely disappeared.

RD'S HAT

THE SECRET

You need an extra piece of the coloured paper, which you cut into a circle and glue to the mouth of the glass as shown in the illustration.

Now if you follow the actions described at the beginning, the trick almost works itself. After you have picked up the glass and hat together, placed them over the coin, and then removed the hat, the coin will be hidden under the secret extra circle of paper.

SPECIAL GLASS

ORDINARY GLASS

MAT COLOUR MATCHES PAPER DISK

Make sure that you trim the paper very carefully level with the rim of the glass, so that when you put the glass upside down on the paper no-one will suspect the extra piece. The wizard's hat is made from stiff paper, and must be just large enough to cover the glass completely. Decorate it with a gold moon and stars to make it look really magical.

The most important thing to remember is that the hat must always be placed over the glass before you move it.

Two more tips. Firstly, it's a good idea to leave another similar glass lying around so that suspicious people can see that it is quite ordinary, and secondly, always use a thin coin for this trick, since a thick coin might show as a lump under the paper.

SEEING THE COLOURS

Would you like to prove that you have X-ray eyes like Superman? Here is one way that you can do it.

You need five small opaque envelopes, and five plain white post cards. On each of the cards you must paint or crayon a different coloured spot. These are all handed out to your audience, and you ask them to fold the cards, with the coloured spots on the inside so that they cannot be seen, mix them around, and then put one card in each of the envelopes. Now you show a large brown envelope to be empty,

FOLDED CARD

FIVE OPAQUE ENVELOPES (TWO SETS)

POSTCARDS WITH COLOURED SPOTS (TWO SETS)

and ask for the small envelopes to be mixed thoroughly, then dropped inside.

Putting the large envelope behind your back, you reach inside it and take out one of the small envelopes. Holding it up to your forehead, you concentrate for a few moments, then say, "With my super sixth sense I can see that this envelope contains the colour green". One of the spectators is invited to open it and show that it does indeed contain the green spotted card. You repeat this with the other envelopes, and each time you guess the colour correctly.

SECRET FLAP CUT FROM ANOTHER ENVELOPE

LARGE MANILA ENVELOPE

THE SECRET

There are really two sets of small envelopes and cards. One set is hidden inside a secret compartment in the large envelope. These are arranged beforehand in an order that you have carefully memorised. Of course, these are the envelopes that you bring out one by one. Since you know the order, you can announce the correct colour every time.

The special large envelope is made by cutting the front side from another similar envelope, and inserting it as shown in the picture. The extra set of small envelopes is hidden between this extra piece and the flap side of the envelope. Then the flap is tucked in, over the extra piece, so that no-one can see the secret preparation.

PERFORMANCE

The envelopes containing the folded cards are mixed by the spectators and dropped into the empty side of the large envelope. As soon as you put it behind your back, you pull out the flap so that you can get at the prepared set, and bring them out one by one to concentrate on and reveal the colour each contains. It is a good idea to bring out the last two envelopes together, and hand them to two spectators. While you announce what colours are in the envelopes they hold, you quietly dispose of the large envelope, which still contains the first set of envelopes.

An easy way to memorise the special order of the colours, is to think of the first letter of each colour and make them into a word. For instance, if you used BLUE, ORANGE, RED, GREEN, and YELLOW, the word would be B-O-R-G-Y.

The Stretching String

SHORT STRING

GLITTER DUST

LONG STRING GOES UP THE
SLEEVE AND INSIDE THE SHIRT

All you need for this amazing trick is a short piece of string about 50 cm long, and a magic salt shaker. The string may be handed out for examination so that your friends can see that is quite ordinary. You take the string and fold it in half, then in half again, and so on, until it is a very small bundle, which you push into your closed right fist. Now with your left hand you pick up the magic salt shaker, and sprinkle some salt over your right fist. Then you take hold of one end of the string, and start to pull it out of your hand. It seems to stretch longer and longer, until it is about four times as long when you started.

The Secret

You will have probably guessed by now that you will need an extra 2 metres length of string. You will also need to wear a ring on the second or third finger of your right hand, and a garment that has long sleeves. One end of the string has a knot tied in it and threaded under the ring, and the remainder is passed up your sleeve, and down inside your shirt or blouse. If you wear a jacket it can go up the sleeve of the jacket, then into your inside jacket pocket.

Now you are ready to perform the trick. Have the short piece of string examined, then take it back and fold it into your hand towards yourself so that no-one can see the end of the long string. Close the right fist and push the bundle inside.

Sprinkle it with magic salt from the shaker, then reach inside the hand to find the knotted end of the long string. Pull it out very slowly, pretending that it is stretching. As soon as it is all the way out, hand it to a spectator to examine. Keep the small bundled piece hidden in your right hand. A good way to get rid of it is to pick up the magic salt shaker with the same hand, and drop it into your magic box or pocket, together with the string. Everybody should be too busy examining the long string to notice.

You may wonder what is a 'magic salt shaker'? Well it's really just an ordinary glass saltcellar, containing ordinary salt. But to make it really special you could fill it with glitter dust that you can buy from an arts and crafts shop.

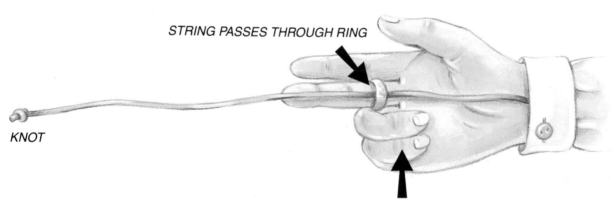

STRING PASSES THROUGH RING

KNOT

BUNDLE OF SHORT STRING
HIDDEN UNDER FINGERS

The Magic Bank

Who wouldn't like to make their money double, just by waving a magic wand? Here is how you can seem to do just that.

Your audience is shown a small plate or tray, on which you can count a number of coins, then ask someone to add up the values. Now you display an empty paper bag on which is written "THE MAGIC BANK". The coins are tipped from the plate into the bag, and the bag given to a spectator to play the part of the bank manager, looking after your investment. You wave your magic wand over him a couple of times, then ask him to tip out the coins, back on to the plate. Imagine his surprise to see that the coins have doubled in quantity and value – 100 per cent instant interest.

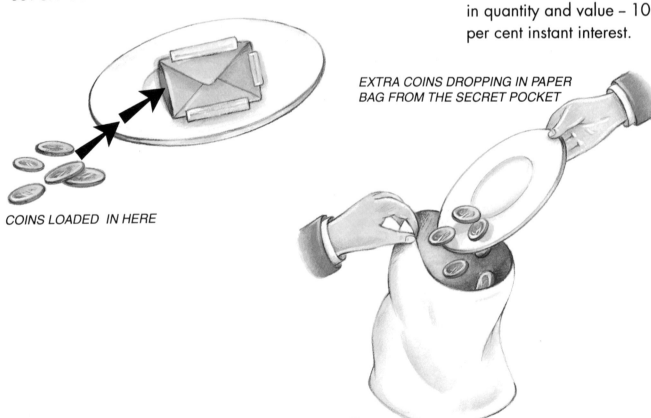

SEALED ENVELOPE WITH END CUT OFF TAPED UNDER PLATE

COINS LOADED IN HERE

EXTRA COINS DROPPING IN PAPER BAG FROM THE SECRET POCKET

The secret

You will need a dozen small coins, which should all be the same value to make it easier to add them up. Also a plate, a thick paper bag, a stiff paper envelope, and some sticky tape. Seal the envelope then cut one end off to make a sort of flat pocket. Fasten this under the plate as shown in the picture, using sticky tape on three sides.

Before your audience arrives insert half the coins carefully into the secret pocket, so that they don't overlap each other, then place the plate gently on the table, with the remainder of the coins on top.

Performance

Pick up the plate with your hand underneath covering the open side of the secret pocket, and tip the coins on the plate into your other hand. Be sure to keep the underside of the plate away from the view of the audience. Now count the coins back on to the plate and let someone add up and remember the total value. Put the plate down for a moment while you show everyone the empty bag. Now pick up the plate again, but this time make sure that the secret pocket opening is pointing towards the bag. Put the edge of the plate part of the way into the bag, and tip it up so that the coins on the top slide into the bag. Of course the coins in the secret pocket slide into the bag at the same time.

Put the plate down, close up the top of the bag and hand it to a spectator. The secret work is now over, and all you have to do is give your 'bank manager' a touch with the magic wand, ask him to tip all the coins out and count them back on the plate – then thank him for doubling your money.

THE COLOU
CHANGIN

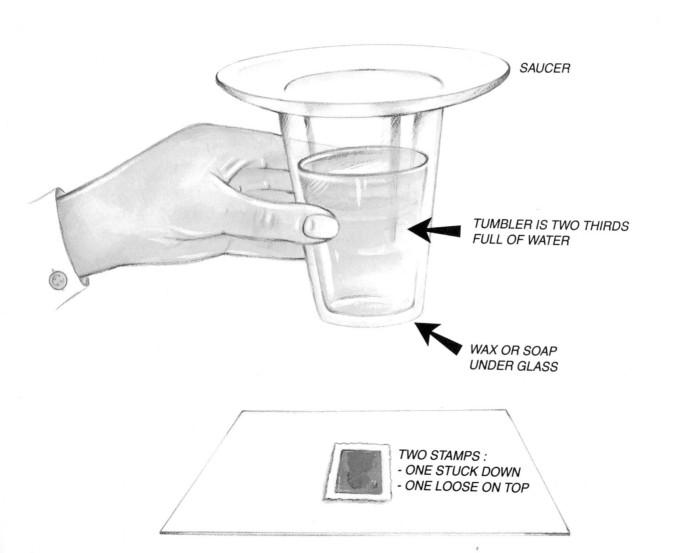

SAUCER

TUMBLER IS TWO THIRDS
FULL OF WATER

WAX OR SOAP
UNDER GLASS

TWO STAMPS :
- ONE STUCK DOWN
- ONE LOOSE ON TOP

STAMP

This is a trick that starts out as an optical illusion, but finishes with a big surprise. You show an envelope on which is stuck a postage stamp. Now you take a glass, fill it about two thirds full of water, and place a saucer on top. Very carefully you lower the glass to cover the stamp. Amazingly the stamp completely disappears. This is due to the fact that the refraction of the water makes the stamp invisible. If you could look straight down into the water from the top of the glass you would see the stamp clearly, but the saucer prevents that and changes the angle of vision. Some of your friends may realise that it is just an optical illusion, but you fool them completely when you lift up the glass, and they see that the stamp has changed colour!

The secret

You need an envelope or post card with a stamp stuck to it, positioned in the middle rather than its usual place in the corner. You will have guessed by now that you will need another stamp, the same size, but a completely different colour. Try to get a good contrast of colours. This extra stamp is placed very carefully on top of the first stamp so that no-one can tell that there are really two stamps. Underneath the bottom of the glass you need to place a dab of something slightly sticky, like wax, or lip salve, or you can rub a piece of wet soap over it just before you do the trick.

Performance

Show your friends the envelope, which should be already on the table or a tray, so as not to disturb the loose stamp. Make sure that they notice the colour of the stamp. You could start by asking them if they know the colour of that particular value stamp, then show them the stamp as if to give the answer.

Then place your glass, with the saucer on top, down over the stamp, and announce that the stamp has completely disappeared. Let everyone see that what you say appears to be true, then lift the glass. Due to the sticky stuff the loose stamp sticks to the bottom of the glass, leaving the different colour stamp in view to amaze your friends. While they are busy examining the stamp stuck to the envelope you may secretly slide the loose stamp off the bottom of the glass, and get rid of the evidence.

You may have to experiment with different glasses to find which one works the best. Usually, a straight-sided tapered tumbler, as illustrated, will be found to work well.

Here is a really easy way to find a playing card that has been chosen by a spectator, then mixed back into the pack. Before you show the trick sort out the cards into reds and blacks. Put all the red cards on the top of the pack, and all the black cards on the bottom.

Find the CARD

ALL RED CARDS ON TOP - BLACK CARDS ON BOTTOM

Performance

Hold the cards face down and spread the top half for someone to take a card. Of course it will be a red one. While your victim is looking at it and showing it to his friends, close the cards together, and then spread out the bottom half. Ask for the card to be replaced, and naturally it will go into the black half. Now you can ask for the pack to be cut a few times (NOT shuffled), so that you do not actually disturb the order of the pack. Now all you have to do is look through the pack to find the one red card amongst the black ones.

After the trick is over it is a good idea to shuffle the cards so that your special arrangement cannot be discovered.

SPECTATOR CHOOSES A CARD FROM TOP HALF - CHOSEN CARD GOES BACK INTO BOTTOM HALF

The Creepy Ball

This is a really spooky trick to watch. In fact, if you turn the lights down low or perform the trick by candle-light, it can give your audience a weird feeling. It's an ideal trick for Halloween.

Here's what happens. You are sitting at a table, covered with a cloth, and with people sitting around it. You let them examine an ordinary table tennis ball, which you place in the centre of the table. You wiggle your fingers over the ball, and mutter some mystical words. Slowly the ball starts to move across the table, all by itself. You command it to stop and start again, and it does as it is told.

Now you place on the table a little tunnel made from folded cardboard. More finger wiggling, and you tell the ball to move and stop, and it obeys perfectly. After the trick is over you can let your audience examine both the ball and the tunnel to their heart's content. There is nothing to find.

How it's done

You need a length of strong thread, and a small curtain or key ring. Tie one end of the thread to the ring, pass the other end around the table, and tie it to the opposite side of the ring, to make a continuous loop over and under the table top. The picture shows exactly how it should look before you cover it with the table-cloth, which should be soft but not too thick. You must sit close to the edge of the table, so that you can reach under the cloth.

One idea you might like to try is to fix the thread loop to your knee with a safety pin, so that you can work the trick by moving your knee from side to side. This leaves both hands free to be seen above the table top.

Also you might like to paint the ball with strange stripes, to make it a little more intriguing. You could even try luminous paint, and turn the lights right off. It's all up to you to create a spooky atmosphere.

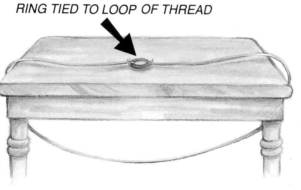

RING TIED TO LOOP OF THREAD

CARDBOARD TUNNEL

OTHER HAND PULLS LOOP UNDER TABLE

On the table are displayed two wine glasses, two sheets of coloured tissue paper, one red, one blue, and two dice of the same colours. The magician picks up the RED die, wraps it in the BLUE paper, then drops the package into one of the glasses. Then the BLUE die is wrapped in the RED paper, and dropped into the second glass.

Now the magician taps each glass with his magic wand, and orders the dice to change places. When the dice are unwrapped the RED one is in the RED paper, and the BLUE one is in the BLUE paper.

HOW IT'S DONE

Apart from the objects already mentioned, you will need an extra BLUE die, and a little bit of sleight of hand. Before the trick starts you hide this extra blue die in the curled third and little fingers of your hand ((see the picture), and proceed as follows.

1 Pick up the sheet of BLUE paper in your left hand and the RED die between thumb and first finger of your right hand.

2 Pretend to wrap the RED die into the paper, but really change the dice over, so that it is the BLUE one that gets wrapped, and RED one goes into hiding, curled inside your third and little fingers. This secret move happens behind the paper so there is no danger of the audience seeing it.

3 Drop the package into one of the glasses.

4 Pick up the RED paper in the left hand, and the BLUE die between thumb and first finger of the right hand, in which you still have the RED die hidden.

5 Pretend to wrap the BLUE die in the RED paper, but really substitute the hidden RED one. Get the BLUE die into the secret hiding place in your fingers, and drop the package into the second glass.

6 Remind your audience that you have wrapped each of the dice in the OPPOSITE coloured papers. This is very important.

7 Pick up the magic wand in your right hand, and tap the two glasses. Then put the wand away out of sight together with the hidden blue die.

8 All that remains to do is to unwrap the packages to show that the dice have changed places and are now in matching papers.

Instead of dice you can use any small objects, such as balls of wool, checkers, draughts, wrapped candies, or even small model animals, and of course they don't have to be red and blue – any contrasting colours will do.

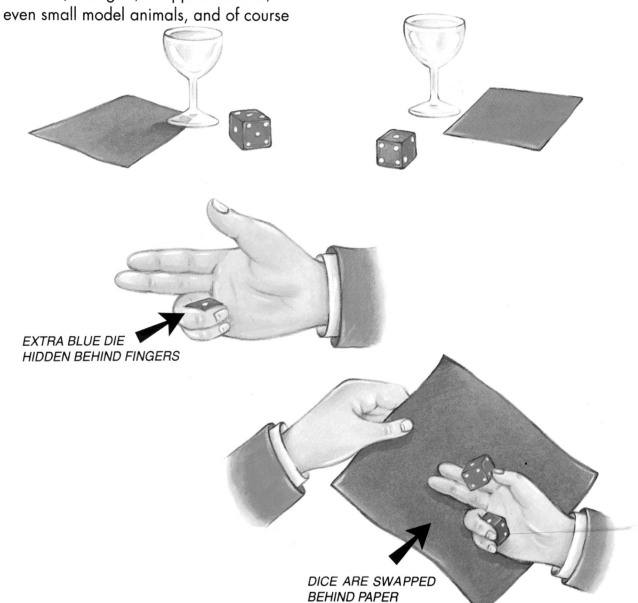

EXTRA BLUE DIE HIDDEN BEHIND FINGERS

DICE ARE SWAPPED BEHIND PAPER

WHAT'S FO

Do you have trouble trying to decide what you would like to eat for lunch? In this trick you can let a friend have a free choice of three different meals, yet you can prove that you knew in advance which one would be chosen.

You need three pieces of plain card about the size of a postcard, three opaque envelopes, one large brown envelope, and paints or crayons. On the first card draw a picture of a hamburger. On the back of the card, in bold letters, write – 'YOU WILL CHOOSE THE HAMBURGER'. Put the card into an envelope, picture side up.

On the second card draw a plate of fish and chips. Leave the back of the card blank. Place it in an envelope, and write on the FACE of the envelope – 'YOU WILL CHOOSE THE FISH AND CHIPS'.

On the third card draw a plate of spaghetti, leave the back blank and place the card into the last small envelope. On the FRONT side of the large brown envelope write – 'YOU WILL CHOOSE SPAGHETTI'.

Before the show, place the large envelope on the table, writing side down, and slide the small envelopes into it with their flap sides upwards.

REVERSE SIDE

YOU WILL CHOOSE THE HAMBURGER!

HAMBURGER

BLANK ON BACK

FISH & CHIPS

YOU WILL CHOOSE THE FISH & CHIPS!

FRONT OF ENVELOPE

SPAGHETTI

ENVELOPES MUST BE OPAQUE

R LUNCH

PERFORMANCE

Slide the small envelopes out one by one, being careful not to let anyone see the writing on the front of the 'fish and chips' envelope. Open each envelope and pull the pictures part of the way out so that your friends can recognise each of the three meals. Push them back into the envelopes, close the flaps, place them on top of the large envelope, and mix them around a bit so that no-one knows which is which (it doesn't matter if they do – the trick will still work).

Now you ask a member of your audience to point to one of the envelopes. Emphasise that the choice is quite free. Open the flap and pull out the chosen card. If it is the HAMBURGER ask the spectator to hold the card face up while you take out the other two cards (carefully keeping the envelopes face down). Then turn over your two cards to show the backs are blank. When the chosen HAMBURGER card is turned over your friend will be surprised to see you have correctly predicted the choice.

If the FISH AND CHIPS card is chosen, show it briefly but leave the other

cards in the envelopes. Then turn all the envelopes over so that everyone can see that only one has writing on the front side predicting the correct choice.

If the SPAGHETTI card is chosen, take it out of the envelope, and put the others aside. Then turn over the large envelope to show the message.

Of course, you should never show this trick to the same audience twice, or they may be able to work out how it is done.

MESSAGE ON FRONT OF LARGE ENVELOPE

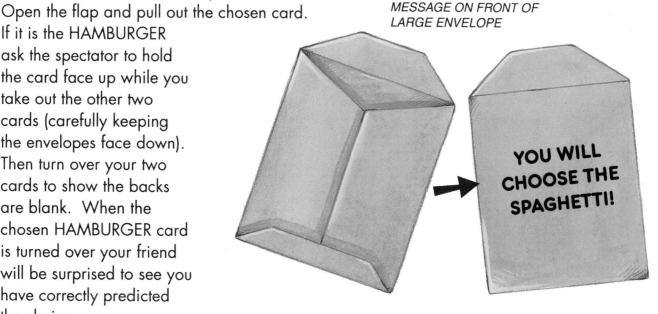

YOU WILL CHOOSE THE SPAGHETTI!

THE GREAT ROBBERY

The magician tells a story about a girl who buys a bottle of lemonade. The bottle is wrapped in brown paper and put into an empty carrier bag. While she is waiting for a bus a wicked lemonade thief steals the bottle out of the bag and hides it by wrapping it in his newspaper. When the girl gets home she finds her bag empty. Luckily she knows a magic word or two, and soon the thief finds that the stolen bottle has disappeared, only to reappear inside the girl's carrier bag.

X-RAY VIEW OF CARRIER BAG SHOWING FAKE HELD IN BY CLIP

RECEIPT FALLING OUT

Requirements

You need a small full bottle of lemonade, two sheets of thick brown wrapping paper, a small paper carrier bag –

FAKE BOTTLE MADE FROM BROWN PAPER AND TAPE

the kind that has a flat bottom, a small slip of paper representing the receipt from the shop, a paper-clip, and some sticky tape.

Preparation

First you must make a fake parcel that looks like a wrapped bottle. The way to do this is to take one of your sheets of wrapping paper and wrap it around the bottle, pressing it in firmly so that it takes on the shape of the bottle. Trim the bottom of the paper so that you can take the bottle out, then maybe strengthen the bottom edge with an extra strip of paper pasted inside.

The paper-clip is fixed to the inside of the carrier bag near the bottom. The bottom edge of the fake bottle shape is clipped to this so that the carrier bag may be tipped upside down without the fake falling out. Drop the paper receipt into the bag, and you are all set.

LEMONADE

Performance

As you tell the story you tip the bag upside down to let the receipt fall out, which 'proves' that the bag is empty without actually saying so. Put the receipt back. Then you wrap the real bottle with your second sheet of brown paper. Try to make it look as much like the fake bottle as possible. Put the wrapped bottle into the bag next to the fake. When you tell them about the thief stealing the bottle, you take out the fake bottle and wrap it in a sheet of newspaper. Don't forget it is supposed to be a real bottle with some weight. Place it on the table to one side.

When you get to the part where the girl arrives home, you grasp the carrier bag at the bottom, gripping the bottle inside at the same time, and turn the bag upside down. The receipt falls out once again 'proving' the bag to be empty. Turn the bag right side up again and place it down for a moment. Go over to the fake newspaper parcel and crush it firmly into a ball – the thief's stolen bottle has vanished. Finally go back to the carrier bag and show that the bottle of lemonade has returned.

BUS STOP

THE REAL WRAPPED BOTTLE IS STILL IN THE BAG!

THE GENIE IN

The magician shows a small opaque bottle, and tells the audience that it contains a mysterious genie. He takes a shoelace that has been tied into a loop, and dangles it into the neck of the bottle. He commands the genie to take hold of the shoelace. When he lifts the lace the bottle is lifted with it – just as if someone inside was hanging on tightly to the loop. Then the genie is ordered to let go, and the bottle comes free of the lace.

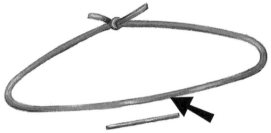

5cm WIRE INSERTED INTO SHOELACE

Requirements

You need a small opaque plastic bottle with a narrow neck like that in the picture – the sort that is sold containing hair shampoo or hand lotion. Scrape the printing off with a wire wool cleaning pad, then stick on some some stars to make it look more magical.

Also you require a pair of long shoelaces – the sort that have a hollow centre. Secretly prepare one of these by pushing a used match or length of wire into the centre as shown. This is easy if the lace

has a loose weave. Tie both laces into a loop, but put the unprepared one aside for the moment.

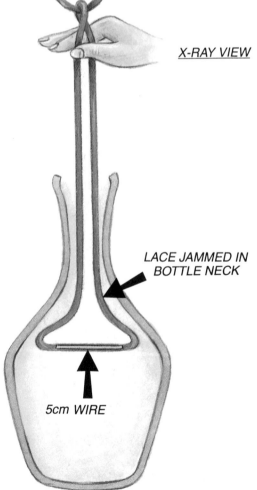

X-RAY VIEW

LACE JAMMED IN BOTTLE NECK

5cm WIRE

THE BOTTLE

Performance

Show the bottle and tell your audience about your tame genie (or he could be a leprechaun or a little goblin). Take hold of the shoelace loop at the point marked 'X' so that the wired section is hanging straight downwards. Then lower the loop well down into the bottle. Now raise the loop by taking hold of the knot with your other hand and lifting gently. The wired bit will now turn sideways and jam in the neck of the bottle, as you can see in the X-ray picture.

Now you could even dare swing the bottle round and round, but the genie will not let go. It's quite safe provided that you hold on to the knot. Finally you let the bottle rest on the table and lift the loop out by holding it a little way below the knot, which turns the wire upright again, and allows the loop

to come free of the bottle.

After the performance is over you can leave the bottle lying around together with the unprepared loop, and watch your friends trying in vain to make the trick work.

X

INSTANT RABBIT

Magicians often get asked "Can you produce a rabbit out of a hat?". Here's a little gadget that you can carry in your pocket to do just that. You show a small picture of a top hat in a frame, with a question mark over the hat. Then, quick as a wink, the question mark changes instantly into a cute little rabbit.

You require a piece of stiff paper or thin card about 20cm by 9cm. Cut little flaps as shown by the dotted lines. Get a grown-up to help you do this with a sharp craft knife. Then copy the picture of the rabbit in the hat onto the lower half of the paper. The frame around the hat is to disguise the edges of the flap, and the top of the hat should be exactly along the cut edge.

Now fold the top half backwards behind the lower half, along the line and tuck the

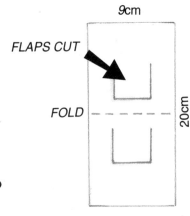

FLAPS CUT

FOLD

9cm

20cm

the lower half, along the line and tuck the little flaps one inside the other, so that the rabbit is now hidden by the back flap. Draw a large question mark on this so that it looks like the illustration.

PERFORMANCE

Show the picture, and tell your friends to watch the hat closely. Now open and close the folded paper VERY QUICKLY. The flaps will pull out from each other, and the question mark will change instantly to the rabbit.

You can employ this idea to make a beautiful face change to an ugly one, or a toad change to a handsome prince. All it needs is a little imagination to work out your own transformation.

*PICTURE FRAME DISGUISES
EDGE OF FLAP*

*DOTTED LINE SHOWS
THE CUT FLAP*

*BACK FLAP TUCKED IN
FRONT OF FRONT FLAP*

*TWO HALVES PULLED APART
QUICKLY TO MAKE THE RABBIT
APPEAR*

TURNOVER CARDS

Performance

The magician spreads a pack of cards face down on the table and asks three people each to select a card, look at it, and remember it. The pack is gathered together and the three cards are pushed back into it, one near the top, one in the middle, and one near the bottom. Now the pack is wrapped in a handkerchief, and the magician taps the bundle three times with a magic wand. When the pack is unwrapped, and the cards spread out again face down on the table, the three chosen cards have turned FACE UP!

Spread the cards face down on the table and ask three people to each take out a card and look at it. While they are doing this you scoop the cards back into a pack. Ask the spectators to show their cards to each other, but not to you. While their attention is distracted you secretly turn the pack completely over so that the double-backed card is on top.

Keep the cards neatly squared together and ask the spectators to push their cards back face-down into the pack, in different places. Be careful not to let the cards spread, or they will see that your cards are really face up.

Now wrap the cards in a handkerchief or a piece of tissue paper. This gives you the chance to turn the pack back over secretly, so that all the cards – except for the chosen ones - are now face down again. Three taps with the magic wand, then unwrap the pack and spread the cards out on the table to show that the three chosen cards have turned themselves over, and are now face up.

GLUE THE JOKERS TOGETHER FACE TO FACE

Preparation

Take the two jokers out of the pack, and glue them carefully face to face, to make what magicians call a double-backed card. Put this card at the bottom of the face-down pack.

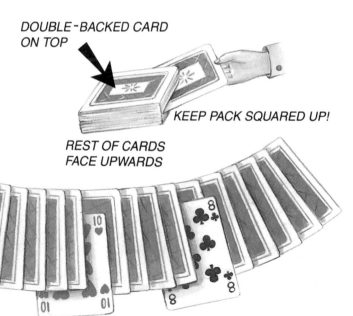

DOUBLE-BACKED CARD ON TOP

KEEP PACK SQUARED UP!

REST OF CARDS FACE UPWARDS

ONE LUMP OR THREE?

This easy bit of magic starts out as a joke, but finishes with a surprise. You will need some sugar lumps, a cup, a saucer, and a little practise.

First, you show the cup to be quite empty, then take two sugar lumps and drop them in, counting "One, two!" You put the saucer on top of the cup to prevent the lumps from escaping. Now you pick up another lump, and say that you will make it completely vanish. You mutter some magic words, and wiggle your fingers over it, but it doesn't disappear. So you say, "We will adopt plan B," then pop the sugar lump in your mouth and eat it.

Your friends will probably say that is cheating, and not much of a trick. So you tell them that you will make it come back into the cup. When you lift off the saucer, and pour the lumps, there are now three instead of two.

How it's done

Before you start, hide a lump of sugar in your hand, with the third and little fingers curled around it. Don't squeeze it tightly, just hold the hand loosely, then no-one will suspect you are one ahead. When you pick up the two lumps, take one with each hand, holding them between thumbs and first fingers. As you drop them together into the cup, you let the

hidden one drop in as well. Then you quickly cover the cup to prevent anyone taking a sneaky look inside. The secret work is now done, and the rest is easy. Just follow the description above.

EXTRA LUMP OF SUGAR HIDDEN UNDER FINGERS

Instead of sugar lumps you can do it with small wrapped sweets, or those coloured chocolate beans, but make sure that the one you eat is the same colour as the extra one you have secretly added. Grapes or

HIDDEN LUMP OF SUGAR DROPPED INTO CUP ALONG WITH VISIBLE SUGAR LUMPS

strawberries could also be used, and they have an advantage in that they don't rattle.

This is a good trick if you have a sweet tooth, but always remember to clean your teeth thoroughly afterwards.

THE VANISH!

KNOTS AWAY

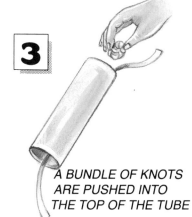

A BUNDLE OF KNOTS ARE PUSHED INTO THE TOP OF THE TUBE

Sometimes there are tricks which work by themselves, and you don't know exactly how they work. You just have to follow the instructions carefully, and the magic just happens. For this one you need a long piece of soft string or thin ribbon, and a cardboard tube, the sort you find when a roll of paper kitchen towels is used up. You can make the tube look more attractive by painting it or covering it with gift wrapping paper.

What happens

First you make a knot near one end of the string, put the tube into it, and pull the knot tight. Then you tie some more knots along the tube. The picture shows you exactly how it should look (1). The formation of each knot must be precisely the same. Now you hold the tube upright, and thread the top end of the string down through the tube (2). Next you must slide the knots all together, then up and off the top of the tube. They will form a little bundle, which you push inside the top of the tube.

Ask someone to take hold of each end of the string and pull it tight. Now you may slide the tube back and forth along the string to show that the knots have completely vanished. The nice thing about this trick is that it is quite automatic. The knots actually dissolve away as you push them into the tube. Ask your friends to guess where they go to.

DICE DIVINATION

I hope you are good at adding and subtracting numbers in your head, because that is what you need to be able to do for this amazing feat of divination using three dice. Fortunately the sums that you have to do are not very big ones.

WHAT HAPPENS

While you turn your back you ask someone to pile up the three dice into a stack in any order they wish. When you turn round, you point out that there are five sides of the dice that you cannot see – underneath the top one, the top and the bottom of the middle die and the top and bottom of the lowest one. You say that by concentrating hard you can tell what is the total of the numbers on those hidden sides. You announce the number, and when the five unseen sides are totalled your audience will be amazed to find you are correct.

You may repeat the trick several times, and each time there can be a different result, but your mental calculations are always correct.

HOW IT'S DONE

The first thing you do when you turn round is to look at the number on the top side of the top die, then subtract that number from twenty-one. The answer will be the total of the hidden sides. It always works.

THE SECRET

The opposite sides of a die always total seven – six and one – five and two – and four and three. So naturally the tops and bottoms of three dice will total twenty-one. Taking away the only visible number on the top die will give you the total of all the hidden numbers.

SUBTRACT THIS NUMBER FROM 21

THE FIVE HIDDEN SIDES ADD UP TO 17

21-4=17

LOOPY LOOPS

Now for a very quick surprising trick which almost works itself. You need two differently coloured pieces of ribbon or thick wool, each about 40cm long. Tie each one into a circle, with as neat a knot as you can manage. Let us say that one is red and the other yellow – the colours should contrast as much as possible.

Put the red loop through the yellow one, and bring both ends together, leaving the yellow loop dangling from the centre. Now pass a pencil or stick through both ends of the red loop, and get someone to hold each end of the pencil.

Explain that it would be impossible to get the red loop off the pencil by pulling on the yellow loop, and

PULL HERE

you prove this to be true by giving it a good tug – nothing happens. Now place your hand around both loops and slide your hand down to the bottom of the yellow loop, saying "One!". Repeat the action, saying "Two!". Now repeat it once more, saying "Three!", but this time you get hold of one side of the red loop and pull it firmly downwards as far as it will go. An amazing thing happens. The red loop now becomes the lower loop, and the yellow loop finishes up doubled round the pencil – somehow they have changed places, then pull the yellow loop to get the red loop to go back to where it started.

THE MAGNE

It's always great fun if you can lead your audience on to think that they know how a trick is done. Then baffle them completely by using another secret method!

THE AUDIENCE'S VIEW

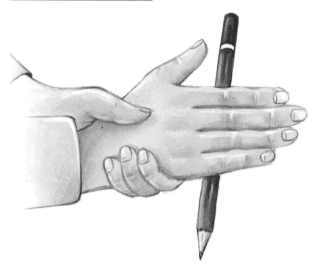

What they will see

You take an ordinary pencil in your right hand, while your left hand rubs your right wrist – "to create the magnetic force". Then you open your right hand, with its back to the audience, and the pencil seems to cling to the fingers just as if it was magnetised.

Unfortunately your friends may be suspicious of the left hand, which is still holding your right wrist. So you give in and let them see how it is done, by turning the right palm towards them. Then they will see that you have extended the left forefinger to keep the pencil in place.

"But if I was a real magician," you say, "I would be able to take my finger away like this!" And believe it or not, the pencil still stays clinging to your hand. Then you can pull it off and hand it to them for examination without them being able to discover the secret.

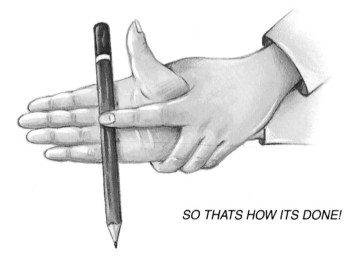

SO THATS HOW ITS DONE!

TIC PENCIL

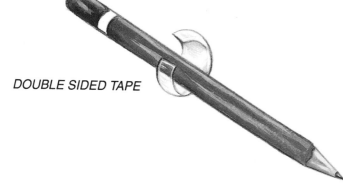

DOUBLE SIDED TAPE

How it's really done

All you need is a short piece of narrow transparent sticky tape. Before the show, you carefully wrap this tape around the pencil WITH THE STICKY SIDE OUT. It will stick to itself to form an almost invisible sleeve which will slide up and down the pencil. It should fit as tightly as possible.

Performance

Hold the pencil in your right hand, and go through the business of rubbing your wrist. When you open your right hand you stick out your left forefinger, which keeps the pencil in place, and also hides the tape. When you have turned your hand around to show 'How it's done', turn it back again so that the back of the hand is towards the audience. Press hard with your left forefinger so that the pencil really sticks to the right hand, then take away the left hand. The pencil stays in position, held by the sticky tape.

Finally, close your hand, slide the pencil out, and give it to someone, leaving the sticky sleeve hidden in your hand. Wait for a moment when no-one is looking to get rid of it into your pocket. If anyone asks you to repeat the trick, just say that the magnetic effect only lasts for a short time – and do another trick.

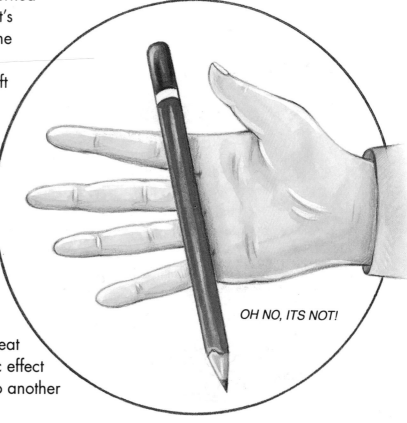

OH NO, ITS NOT!

39

MAGIC MONEY PAPERS

Would you like to turn silver into gold? Well we can't quite manage that with this trick, but we can turn copper into silver.

What happens

You show a small copper coin and wrap it in a square of coloured paper. This is then wrapped in a slightly larger square of paper, which in turn is wrapped in a yet larger square. When the papers are unfolded again, the coin has changed to a silver one.

Requirements

You will actually need five squares of paper. One large square 21cm by 21cm. Two middle sized squares 15cm by 15cm. Two small squares 10cm by 10cm. Each square should be a distinctly different colour,

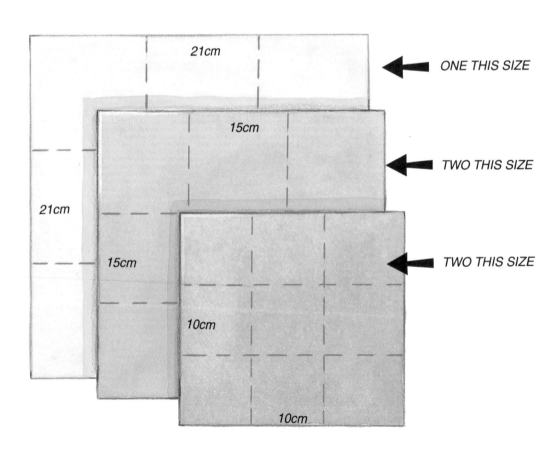

21cm

ONE THIS SIZE

15cm

TWO THIS SIZE

21cm

15cm

10cm

TWO THIS SIZE

10cm

and patterned paper helps to hide the secret. Fold each square carefully into three each way, as shown by the dotted lines in the picture. Then take the two middle sized papers in a folded condition, turn one over, and glue them back to back, being very careful to put glue only on the middle square section of the papers. Do this as neatly as possible so that the edges match all round, and either way up it should look like a single folded paper.

Preparation

Fold a small silver coin into one of the smallest squares, then fold that into one side of the special middle paper, and turn it over. Keep the other side open and uppermost, and place it on the unfolded large square. On top of this place the remaining small square, also opened up. Have a small copper coin at the ready.

Performance

Show the copper coin and wrap it in the small square. TURN THE PACKET OVER and place it in the centre of the middle square. Fold this up and TURN THE PACKET OVER. Now mutter some mystic words such as "Wishee washee wolla wolla wom pom pom!", turn the packet over again, and unfold the large paper – leaving it on the table as you do so. Do likewise with the middle paper. Pick up the smallest packet, and hand it to someone to unfold. They will be surprised to find that the copper coin has changed to a silver one. If you follow the actions exactly as I have described them the trick works quite automatically.

These magic money papers are very useful. As well as changing money they can be used to make any small flat object appear, vanish, or change. Why not combine it with the Colour Changing Stamp Trick.

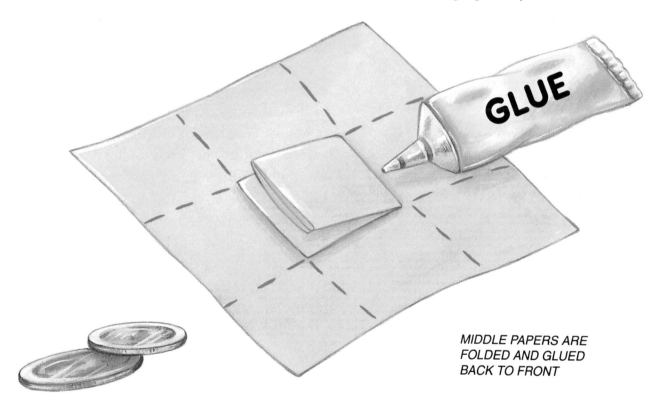

MIDDLE PAPERS ARE
FOLDED AND GLUED
BACK TO FRONT

ABRACADABRA
- YOUR CARD WAS!

There are few card tricks that are as easy as this one. Just follow the instructions and it all works so mechanically you will surprise yourself, as well as your audience.

WHAT YOU DO

Take an ordinary pack of cards and count off twenty-one cards. Deal three cards face up into a line . Then add a second card to each, then a third, and so on until you have dealt out seven cards to each row as in Figure 1. Every card should be visible. Now ask someone just to THINK of one of the cards, without telling you what it is – only what ROW it is in. Gather up each row into separate packets, being very careful to keep the cards in the same order. Put the packet containing the chosen card on top of one of the other packets, and put the third packet on top of that, always keeping the cards face up. It's like making a sandwich of the three packets, with the chosen card packet as the filling.

Now deal the cards out one by one into the rows just as before. Ask the spectator to say which row the chosen card is in. Again gather the three rows, keeping them in order, and put the packet containing the chosen card in between the other two packets. Repeat this whole process ONE MORE TIME. It is very important to remember that the chosen card packet is placed between the other two packets THREE times in all.

Now turn the complete packet of twenty-one cards face down, and start to deal them one by one face down on to the table from the top of the packet. As you deal them you spell out the magic word ABRACADABRA, letter by letter. Say "A" for the first card, "B" for the second, and so on. When you come to the last "A", hold it for a moment, and ask the spectator for the name of the card he thought of. Turn the card in your hand over, and it will be the one named.

If you follow the instructions correctly, the chosen card will always be the eleventh card from the top of the pack, so you could use any word or words like ABRACADABRA that use eleven letters. You could spell ACHEBAZOOKA or YOUR CARD WAS. If you are lucky enough to have eleven letters in your own name you could use that. If not, try making up your own magic words.

Figure 1.

MAKE SURE THIS CARD
IS VISIBLE IN THE SPREAD

ZIPPETY CLIPS

You will be very surprised when you try out this little stunt. And the strange thing is, I cannot really tell you how it works – it just does!

1

STIFF STRIP OF PAPER

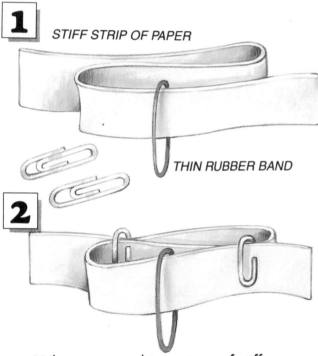

THIN RUBBER BAND

2

What you need is a piece of stiff paper about 30 cm long, and 3 cm wide. If you can't get ribbon, a strip of stiff drawing paper cut to the same size will work just as well. Besides the ribbon you will require two paper-clips, the larger the better, and a thin rubber band.

WHAT YOU DO

Fold the paper into three as in Figure 1, and slide the rubber band over one end as shown. Now take the paper-clips and put one on the left side over the BACK fold and the MIDDLE fold, to hold the two folds together. Put the other clip over the MIDDLE fold and the FRONT fold on the right-hand side. If you study Figure 2 carefully you will see exactly where the clips have to go.

Now you are set to make the magic happen. Take hold of one end of the ribbon in each hand. Say "ONE, TWO, THREE, GO!" and pull the ribbon out straight – firmly but smoothly. The paper-clips will pop-off the ribbon, and not only join themselves to each other, but also to the rubber band, then hang down in a chain from the centre of the ribbon (Figure 3).

How does it work? I don't know!

3

THE Magic Diver

Sometimes magic depends on scientific principles. Here's one you can have a lot of fun with. You will require a plastic cap from a felt tip pen, a plastic lemonade bottle, some modelling clay, a thin nail, and a cup of water.

on. Squeeze the bottle gently, and the diver will start to descend. Squeeze hard, and it will sink right to the bottom. Release the pressure, and the diver will rise again, going back right up to the top. With a little practise you can make it go up

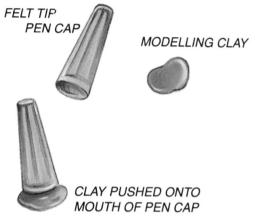

FELT TIP PEN CAP

MODELLING CLAY

X-RAY VIEW

AIR

THIN NAIL TO MAKE A HOLE

CLAY PUSHED ONTO MOUTH OF PEN CAP

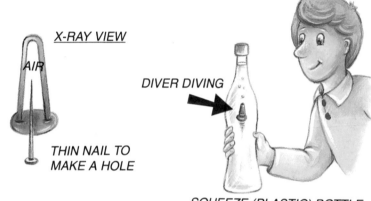

DIVER DIVING

SQUEEZE (PLASTIC) BOTTLE

First take a piece of modelling clay (Plasticine) about the size of a small marble, and knead it until it is quite soft. Then roll it into a ball, and press it on to the opening of the pen cap, so that it is sealed. Drop the cap into the cup of water. If it sinks, fish it out, remove a tiny bit of the clay, and try again. The idea is that you have to adjust the weight of the clay until the pen cap only just floats. It's a fiddly business which will take a little time to get exactly right. You will know when it is perfect, when the top of the pen cap stays just level with the surface of the water, and a tiny touch sinks it for a few moments.

Now take your thin nail, and carefully make a hole in the clay right through to the inside of the cap (see the diagram). Fill the lemonade bottle right to the top with water, drop the diver in, and screw the bottle cap

and down fast or slow, and even hover half-way up.

If it doesn't work at first, you may need to adjust the weight of the clay slightly and always make sure no water has got inside the pen cap.

Another way to make the diver work is to use a glass bottle, with a small balloon tightly stretched over the neck of the bottle. Pressing down on the rubber will control the diver's movements in the same way as squeezing the plastic bottle, but the diver has to be very finely adjusted in this case.

PUSH DOWN

SMALL BALLOON

A MATHEMAT

Ask one of your friends to think of a single digit number.

Then multiply it by 9.

Add the two digits in the answer together.

Add 6 to the total.
Divide the answer by 3.
Remember the result.

Of course, all this calculation must be done secretly, so that you can have no idea of his thought-of number, or the result. Explain that the final answer represents a letter of the alphabet. For example 1 would mean letter A, 2 equals B, 3 equals C, 4 equals D, 5 equals E, 6 equals F, and so on.

Once your friend has worked out what letter the final answer represents, tell him he must think of the name of an animal that starts with that letter. You now pretend to concentrate very hard, then announce that he is thinking of an ELEPHANT!

CAL ANIMAL

How do you know

Well, if you try out the calculations for yourself, you will find that the answer is ALWAYS FIVE. For instance, suppose the number first thought of is SIX.

6 multiplied by 9 equals 54.
5 plus 4 equals 9.
9 plus 6 equals 15.
15 divided by 3 equals 5.
And number 5 equals E.

When you ask anyone to think quickly of an animal starting with letter E, the answer will almost always be ELEPHANT. Unless your friend is a really brainy zoologist and comes up with ECHIDNA or EARTHWORM. EAGLE and EMU don't count because they are birds.

If you change the calculation slightly and add 3 instead of 6, that will give a final total of 4. That means the letter would be D. Ask your friend to think of a country in Europe, and the answer will almost certainly be DENMARK.

A FISHY BUSINESS

Comedy tricks are always a popular part of a magic show, because most people like to laugh as well as be mystified. Here is one you can have a lot of fun with.

You start by showing two large envelopes clearly empty. It is most important that everyone can see this so that they will not be suspicious of the envelope at the end of the trick. Now you display two pictures. One is of a cat, who is not very happy, in fact he looks a bit starved. The other picture is of a rather plump fish. You put one picture into each of the envelopes, and place the

CARDS

CUT OUT TO HELP EXTRICATE THE CARD

ENVELOPES

CAT

FISH

envelopes wide apart on two chairs positioned on each side of the stage or room. You make sure that your audience knows exactly where each picture is, by pulling them out for a last look. Now you tell everyone that you will make the cat and fish change places. You pronounce the magic words "ISHY WISHY, LET'S GET FISHY!" and wave your magic wand about a bit. Going over to the envelope that contains the CAT, you peek inside, without taking the picture out, and

48

say "Yes, the FISH is over here!". Then you do the same to the FISH envelope, saying "Yes, the CAT is over here!".

Your audience will begin to murmur in disbelief, but you carry on regardless. "Ah, but that's the easy part of the trick. The difficult part is to make them go back again. "ABRA-CAT-ABRA!" Another wave of the wand, then you show that the CAT and the FISH have returned to their original envelopes.

By now your audience will be hopping mad, and complaining that you did not show that they had really changed places. So you offer to do the trick again, and this time you do bring the pictures out of the envelopes – starting with the FISH picture. But what a surprise – it has changed to a CAT picture, which has now changed to a FISH SKELETON. "Oh dear!" you say. "They DID change places, but the CAT must have eaten the FISH on the way!"

The secret

It will take a little work to make the props for this trick, but it will be worth the effort. You will need two thick white envelopes, the sort that open at the end. Cut the flaps off, and make a little semicircular cut-out at the open end as shown in the picture. On the front of one envelope you draw a picture of a hungry cat, and the other a fat fish. Put a thick black border round each picture, to help hide the fact that it is really an envelope. Cover the back of each envelope with fancy patterned paper, so that they look like the backs of playing cards.

Now you need two pieces of white card which will just fit into the envelopes, but not too tightly. On one card, you draw a smiling

cat, licking his lips, and on the other card a picture of what is left after the cat has finished his supper. Each picture should have a black border, and patterned paper on the back to match the

BLACK BORDERS ARE IMPORTANT

BACK OF CARDS AND ENVELOPES

envelope pictures.

The large envelopes used are quite ordinary, but they should be thick and completely opaque. If you wish you can print "CAT" on one and "FISH" on the other in big bold letters. It will help the audience remember where the pictures are supposed to be. Prepare for your performance by putting the fishbones card inside the hungry cat envelope, and smiling cat card inside the fat fish envelope.

Performance

This follows the description of the trick exactly as above, until you come to the end. The CAT and FISH pictures do not really change places of course. It's all spoof just to get your audience excited. When you finally take the pictures out, you really pull out the card pictures of the SMILING CAT and the FISHBONES. The semicircular cut-outs make it easier to extract the cards from the envelope pictures which are left out of sight inside the large envelopes. Since you showed these clearly empty at the start, no-one should suspect them, and anyway everyone will be laughing too much to care.

THE PAPER-CLIP CHAIN

The humble paper-clip, which used to be obtainable only in plain metal, can now be bought in an assortment of bright colours, which are ideal for use in this trick.

What happens

You show a paper cup containing a whole lot of paper-clips, which you tip into your hand, then let them fall in ones and twos onto a small tray on the table. This is to let your audience see that they are all quite separate. You also let them see that the paper cup is now quite empty.

Now you lift the tray off the table and shake the clips about a bit, picking up a few of them, and letting them fall back on the tray to rub in the idea that they are all loose, and not joined in any way. You pick up the paper cup in your other hand, tilt the tray so that the clips slide into one corner, and then tip them all into the cup. With a magic wand, or a pencil, you stir the clips in the cup and say "ALDI BORONTI FOSFICO FORMIO", which are very old magic words indeed. Very dramatically you reach into the cup, and pull out a chain of clips – they have all joined together in a magic circle.

Requirements

You need enough paper-clips to make a chain about 60 cm long, and the same number of loose clips. Join the ends so that you have an endless circle. The paper cup is quite ordinary, but you may decorate it with stick-on stars to make it look more magical. The tray is made from the lid of a cardboard gift box turned upside-down. It should measure about 25 cm by 15 cm by 3 cm deep.

CUP WITH LOOSE CLIPS

MAGIC WAND

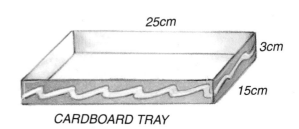

25cm

3cm

15cm

CARDBOARD TRAY

The set up

Before you start your show, place the tray on the table, with a long side towards the audience, and hide the chain along behind the front edge of the tray. Make sure that your audience will be sitting down, and that no-one will be able to get close enough to peer over the edge of the tray. Put the cup containing all loose clips in the centre of the tray. Perhaps it would be a good idea to put a cloth over everything until you begin.

Performance

Pick up the cup, and pour the clips into your hand, explain what they are, and drop them a few at a time onto the tray. Leave a few in the cup, so that you can sprinkle these last clips directly from the cup. Show the cup all round so that everyone can see it is empty. Shake the tray to let the chain mingle with the loose clips, then tip the whole lot back into the cup. If any stray clips miss the cup, just pick them up and drop them in – it helps the illusion. Stir with your magic wand, then reach in with one finger to find the chain. Pull it out slowly, with a little shake to dislodge any loose clips. Display the chain and take your applause. Of course, the loose clips stay in the cup out of sight. Then drop the chain back in the cup to cover the loose clips, and start your next trick.

BIRD'S-EYE VIEW OF THE TABLE SET-UP

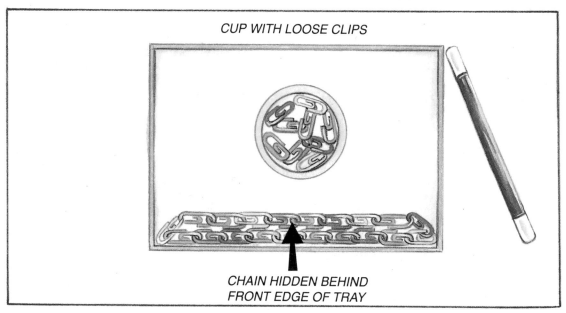

CUP WITH LOOSE CLIPS

CHAIN HIDDEN BEHIND
FRONT EDGE OF TRAY

AUDIENCE

TWO FOR ONE

Have you ever played the game where you hide a coin in one hand, and your companions have to guess which one? This trick starts out just like that, with the guesser always losing, but then it ends in a surprise.

First you show a large coin between the thumb and forefinger of your left hand, while the other hand is clearly empty. Then you close the hands into fists, and bring them together with a sneaky movement, as if you were trying to switch the coin to the other hand. You ask which hand is it in. Your victim says, for example, that it is in the right one. "Wrong!" you say, and open the left hand to show that the coin is there.

Closing your hands again, you bring your fists together, and repeat that sneaky move. Once more you ask your friend to guess, and once again the coin is shown in

the opposite hand to that chosen. Then you tell your audience that they should never take chances with a magician, and open both hands to show you have a coin in each one.

HOW IT'S DONE

The secret is clever but simple like all good tricks. At the start the second coin is hidden behind the first one, by placing it between the left thumb and first finger, pointing straight backwards. In other words its edge is towards the audience. The visible coin is held in front of it with its flat side facing the audience. The first picture shows you exactly how it should look from above, and the second picture shows you the audiences view. The second coin is completely hidden.

When you close your hands into fists and bring them together to make the sneaky move, you must manage to get one coin into each hand. Now when your victims make their guesses all you have to do to prove them wrong is to open the opposite hand.

Finally open both hands for the surprise ending.

Of course, you may prefer to start with the coins in your right hand. Always use the hand with which you are most comfortable.

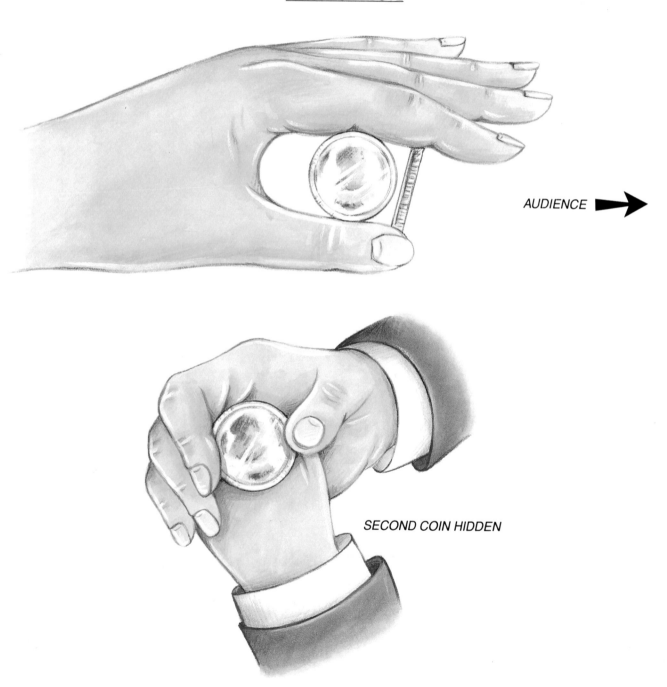

VIEW FROM ABOVE

AUDIENCE ▶

SECOND COIN HIDDEN

HOUDINI
ESCAPES AGAIN

You may have heard of the Great Houdini. He was one of the world's most famous magicians, who specialised in escaping from handcuffs, chains, and all manner of locked boxes and rooms. This trick is dedicated to him.

You show your friends a small paper cut-out of the famous Houdini, and thread him on to the piece of string or ribbon through the spaces inside his elbows. Now, if you get two spectators to each hold one end of the string, there is no way that Houdini can escape.

DARK COLOUR CLOTH

But you explain that he always worked better in the dark, and then cover the cut-out figure with a large dark-coloured handkerchief. Showing your hands completely empty, you reach under the handkerchief and bring out the little paper figure, completely free of the string, and not damaged in any way.

HOW IT'S DONE

The crafty secret is that you need TWO paper Houdinis, one of which is hidden up you sleeve before you start. When both of your hands are out of sight under the handkerchief, you quickly tear the first cut-out off the string, and push it up your right sleeve out of sight. Then you bring out the duplicate from your sleeve, and pull the handkerchief off the string to reveal that the Great Houdini has escaped once again.

I suggest that you make some photocopies of the Houdini cut-outs so that they will all look exactly the same, and you will have enough for several performances.

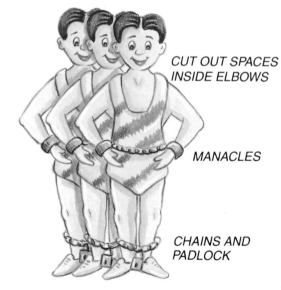

CUT OUT SPACES INSIDE ELBOWS

MANACLES

CHAINS AND PADLOCK

FIVE IN A ROW

This is really a puzzle, but the answer is so tricky it will cause a lot of amusement at a party.

You need five glasses, which you must arrange in a row on the table. Fill the first, third, and fifth glasses with water or lemonade. Now explain to your guests that they have to rearrange the glasses by moving ONLY ONE GLASS, but they must finish up with three full glasses at one end of the row, and two empty glasses at the other.

You will have your friends really scratching their heads over this one, because the more they try the more impossible it will seem.

Finally you put them out of their misery by showing them the tricky solution. Just pick up glass number five from the end, and pour its contents into glass number two, then put it back at the end. Now you have three full glasses at one end and two empty at the other – just as required – and you have only moved ONE GLASS.

PAPER-CLIP PREDICTION

You can use the clips from the 'Paper-Clip Chain' trick for this baffling prediction item. All you need to do is make sure that there are precisely nineteen clips in the chain when you start. Write a prediction on a piece of paper saying 'YOU WILL HAVE EXACTLY NINE CLIPS LEFT'. Fold this up and give it to someone to hold safely. Now hand out your chain of clips to an onlooker, and turn your back so that you cannot possibly see what is about to happen.

Ask the spectator to think of any number from one to eight, and remove that number of clips from the chain. Then ask him to count secretly the number of clips left on the chain. Whatever the answer he has to remove more clips to match the two digits of that answer. For instance, if seven is the number thought of, and removed from the chain, that will leave twelve. He must take one clip from one end, and two clips from the other end. If he thinks of five, that will leave fourteen, which means that one must be taken from one end and four

from the other.

Now open and read your prediction, then count the remaining clips. THE TOTAL WILL ALWAYS BE NINE. Since you could not know what number would be thought of, it seems impossible that you are able to predict the final result.

Two important points to remember. Do not draw attention to the number of clips at the beginning, and always explain very carefully what has to be done, giving an example to make sure your helper makes no mistakes.

START WITH 19 CLIPS (KEEP THE NUMBER SECRET)

5

THINK OF A NUMBER AND TAKE IT AWAY FROM 19

19

The total will always be nine!

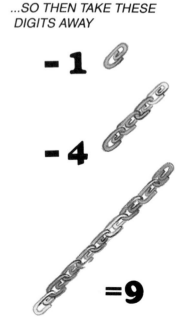

...SO THEN TAKE THESE DIGITS AWAY

-1

-4

=9

PAPER SANDWICH

All you need for this puzzling table trick are three paper serviettes. Two should be white, and the third coloured or patterned to make it recognisable from the other two.

Lay one of the white serviettes diagonally in front of you with one corner pointing towards you. Place the second white one on top, but a little further away, then the coloured one on a little further still, so the result looks like Figure 1. Now start rolling them up together from the corner nearest you, until they are fully rolled.

When you unroll them flat again – surprise, surprise – the coloured serviette will be found sandwiched between the other two. You roll them up once again, and this time when you unroll them the coloured one is at the bottom. Repeat the process one more time and the coloured one jumps back to the top. How did you do it?

It depends on one simple move. When the serviettes are almost completely rolled up, the corner of the bottom serviette will flip over the first, due to the fact that the positions of the serviettes are staggered. Stop rolling immediately when this happens, unroll the serviettes, and you will find the bottom serviette has now become the top one, which causes the coloured one to become sandwiched. Adjust the positions of the serviettes so that they are staggered as at the start, and roll again.

The second time the coloured serviette will arrive at the bottom position, and the third time it will be at the top. If you don't succeed at first, experiment by staggering the serviettes a little bit more.

For a different presentation you could use the squares of writing paper in place of serviettes. Draw a slice of bread on two of the papers, and a splodge of raspberry jam on the third. Then you can tell a story about trying to get the jam in between the slices of bread instead of the top.

BREAD SLICES

RASPBERRY JAM

ROLL FROM THIS END

COLOURED SERVIETTE SANDWICHED INBETWEEN

The PENETRATING Key

Showing your audience a key, you tell them that it has a very strange ability. Not only does it unlock doors, but it also passes through solid objects like a ghost passing through a castle wall. A book is placed on top of a glass tumbler, then another glass on top of that. The key is covered by a handkerchief, and held over the top glass, the key goes through the book, and then lands in the glass beneath.

The secret

You need two glass tumblers, a thick book, a handkerchief, and three flat keys that look exactly the same. One key is tied to a short length of white thread attached to the hem, the other end of which is sewn to the centre of the handkerchief. Before you start, the second key is hidden under the book.

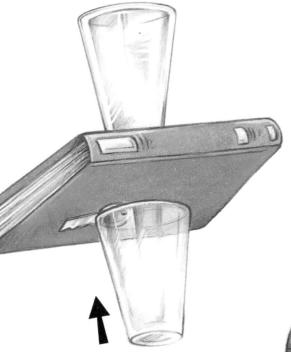

VIEW UNDER THE BOOK SHOWING KEY SECURED BETWEEN THE GLASS AND BOOK

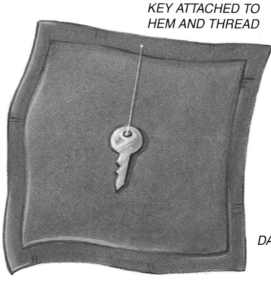

KEY ATTACHED TO HEM AND THREAD

DARK HANDKERCHIEF

Performance

Pick up the book with your fingers underneath to hold key in place, and balance it on the top of the glass, making sure that the key is trapped between the rim of the glass and the book. Put the second glass on top of the book. Show the third key, and pretend to wrap it in the handkerchief. Really, you keep that key in your hand, and push the key on the thread up into the centre of the handkerchief. Ask a spectator to grasp that key through the cloth, and hold it over the glass. While this is happening get rid of the key in your hand.

Ask the spectator to let the handkerchief drop over the glass. The key will fall from the folds of the handkerchief, and everyone will hear it tinkle into the glass. Now you have to do two things at the same time. With one hand you whisk the handkerchief off the glass – with the attached key hidden in its folds – while the other hand lifts the book very slightly, so that the key under it drops in to the lower glass. Any noise made by the handkerchief key leaving the top glass will be disguised by the sound of the second one arriving in the bottom glass.

You quickly put the handkerchief somewhere out of harm's way, separate the book and glasses, tip out the key, and display it as you take your applause.

KEY HIDDEN IN HANDKERCHIEF

BOOK LIFTED SLIGHTLY TO ALLOW KEY TO FALL INTO LOWER GLASS

FOUR CARDS FOUND

I love card tricks in which the spectators do all the work, especially when several people can join in. You ask someone to take your pack of cards and deal it into four face down piles. Four people are requested to select one card each from somewhere in the middle of one of the piles. They may all choose a different pile, but it really does not matter if two or three people pick cards from the same one.

When they have looked at their cards and remembered them – without showing you, of course – tell them to put the cards back on any pile they wish. Again, it really does not matter if more than one card goes on any pile. This apparently haphazard procedure makes the trick all the more baffling and difficult to work out.

Ask them to cut each pile, so that the chosen cards are lost somewhere in the middle of the pile. Then the piles are gathered together in any order to make the pack complete. This can then be cut several times, so that it seems a hopeless task for you to be able to find the chosen cards. Nevertheless you quickly look through the pack and pull out four cards. They prove to be those chosen by the spectators.

HOW IT'S DONE

Before you start, put the four kings on the top of the pack, and the four queens on the bottom. Now when the cards are dealt out into four face-down piles you will end up with a king on the bottom of each pile, and a queen on the top. When each spectator

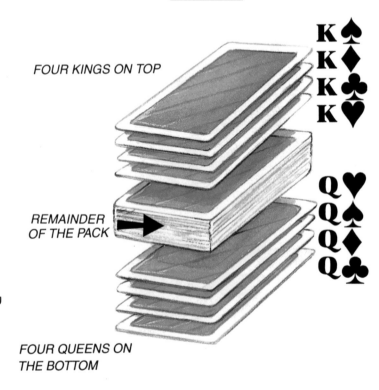

THE SET UP

FOUR KINGS ON TOP

K♠
K♦
K♣
K♥

Q♥
Q♠
Q♦
Q♣

REMAINDER OF THE PACK

FOUR QUEENS ON THE BOTTOM

chooses a card from the middle of a pile, puts it on top, and then cuts the pile, this results in the chosen card being positioned between a king and a queen – a royal sandwich. This happens to all four of the chosen cards in fact. If two cards are replaced on the same sandwich. The reassembling and cutting of the pack does not alter their positions one little bit.

So, when you look through the pack, all you have to do is pick out the four cards between the kings and queens, and they will be the selected cards. It is possible that one of the sandwiches will get split up by the cutting, so should you find a king on the bottom of the pack, look on the bottom for the chosen card. Actually, if you find a king or queen on the top or bottom of the pack it is probably best just to cut the pack one more time to bring the split royals together.

Always make sure that the spectator dealing the cards knows how to deal properly and neatly. Also you may have to explain that cutting a pile or a pack means lifting off about half the cards, putting them down on the table, then completing the cut by placing the bottom half on the top.

K

Q

CARD FROM THE
MIDDLE GOES ON TOP

THE CHOSEN CARD

THE BALANCING BALL

Are you good at balancing things? This magical stunt will make you look like a real expert. You display an ordinary ruler and a table tennis ball. With great concentration you attempt to balance the ball on the end of the ruler. It falls off a few times, but you finally manage to balance it for a few seconds, before you toss it off and catch it in your other hand.

But then you go a stage further. Turning the ruler into a horizontal position, you try to balance the ball on the top edge. After a few failures, you succeed – the ball balances! And now, to the amazement of the onlookers you tilt the ruler slightly, and the ball ROLLS ALONG THE EDGE, then back again – a fantastic feat of juggling!

The secret

You will need a wooden or metal ruler. It is also possible to use a plastic one so long as it is not transparent. Cut a strip of thin cardboard about 2 cm shorter than the ruler and 1 cm narrower, and fix this strip to the back or flat side of the ruler as shown in the picture, using sticky tape. The top edge of the strip should be level with the top edge of the ruler. The tape acts as a hinge, so that the strip of card can be tilted backwards away from the top. If you do this until there is a gap of about 1 cm between the top edges of the strip and ruler, you can put your thumb at the end of the ruler, pressing on the end of the strip so that it stays in that

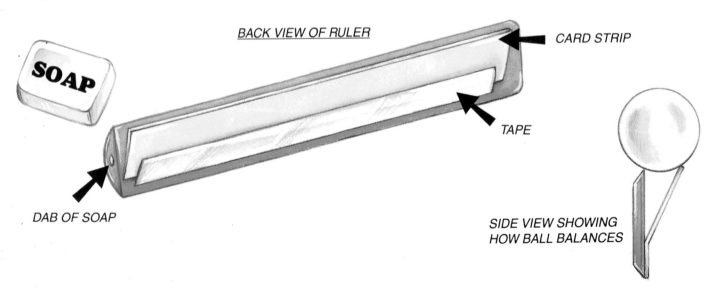

BACK VIEW OF RULER

CARD STRIP

TAPE

SOAP

DAB OF SOAP

SIDE VIEW SHOWING
HOW BALL BALANCES

it stays in that position. You will now be able to balance the ball on top of the two edges, and then let it run from side to side by gently tilting the ruler.

Be careful to keep the ruler above the eyeline of the audience, so that they will not see the cardboard strip, and of course, never let them see the back of the ruler. And remember to act as if it is a really difficult feat to perform. Let the ball drop a few times, then when you succeed the applause will be even greater.

Oh, I nearly forgot to tell you how to balance the ball on the end of the ruler. The answer is simple. Just put a tiny dab of soap or wax in the middle of the end. Press the ball on to this, and it will stick there long enough to make everyone think that the ball is balanced.

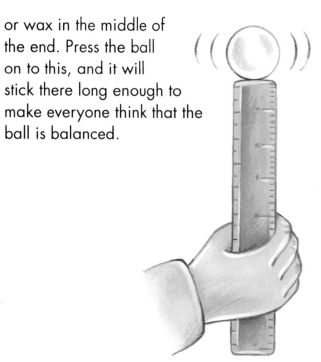

THE FIRST BALANCE

THUMB KEEPS STRIP IN OPEN POSITION

THE THIRSTY SPOOK

THIS PICTURE IS IN THE DARK, MAYBE TAKEN BY INFRA RED

Here's a great trick for a Halloween party. You sit everyone round a table. In front of you there is a wine glass half full of water. Taking a reel of sticky tape, you put strips of it over the mouth of the glass, completely covering the opening. You ask for all the lights to be switched off, as spooks and spirits only come out in the dark. Then you get the person on your left to hold the bottom of the glass with his left hand, and your left wrist with his right hand. You may need to guide his hand to make sure that he doesn't put it on top of the glass. The person on your right does likewise, with right hand on the stem of the glass, and the left grasping your wrist.

With a spooky voice you ask everyone to count from one to thirteen very slowly. Then you call for the lights to be turned on again, and your friends will be amazed to see that the water has disappeared from the glass – apparently consumed by a very thirsty ghost.

THE SECRET

When you cover the glass with the sticky tape you make sure that the edges of the tape do not quite touch, leaving a very small gap in the centre. In your pocket you have a drinking straw. As soon as the lights go out you quickly take out the straw and push it into the glass between the tape strips. Then you can arrange all the hands in position, which seems to prove to everyone that you cannot possibly get at the glass in any way.

As soon as your friends start counting, you lean forward and suck out the water. The counting will cover any noise you may make. As soon as you have finished, you grip the straw between your lips, pull it out of the glass, lean back a bit, and let the straw fall into your lap. Now the evidence is gone, and when the lights are turned back on everyone will be so busy looking at the glass you should have plenty of opportunity to get rid of the straw. A good idea would be to hide a bit of double-sided tape or chewing gum under the edge of the table. Then you could stick the straw to it, completely out of harm's way.

*COVER GLASS
WITH STICKY TAPE*

TOP VIEW

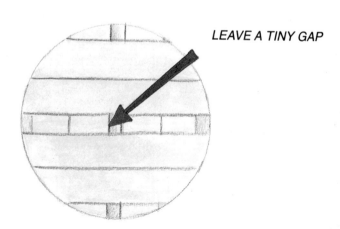

LEAVE A TINY GAP

THE TREASURE CASTLE

One of the most popular themes in magic is to show a sort of container, such as a box, or tube, or bag – which is obviously quite empty – then to bring out all manner of colourful items, like silk handkerchiefs, ribbons and so forth. But even that can be a bit boring, unless you have a good presentation. Here is a production trick that can be dressed up with a story about hidden treasure.

WHAT HAPPENS

Laid flat on your table are some cut-out cardboard pieces decorated to resemble the walls of an ancient castle. You lift them up to show that they are quite thin, and not capable of concealing anything, then you assemble them into a model castle with four walls. This you place on a tray to prove there is no connection with the table.

You tell a story about a prince who lived in the castle, who was very rich, and had lots of gold and jewels. But when he died no-one could find the treasure, because the prince had hidden it in a secret room. One day a clever magician arrived (that's you), and said the well-known words as used by Ali Baba for opening secret doors – 'OPEN SESAME'. Immediately, a hidden panel in the wall creaked open, and there was all the treasure safe and sound inside. Whereupon you produce loads of shiny gold and jewelled objects from inside the model castle.

HOW TO MAKE THE CASTLE

You will require some sheets of poster board, which can be obtained from an art shop. Cut them to the sizes and shapes indicated in the illustration. Ask a grown-up to help you with this because it needs a sharp cutting knife. Notice the two slots in each panel. These are to enable you to assemble them into a box. Paint the panels grey with black lines, to look like the walls of an ancient castle.

Now you must make a secret load box, which is hinged to the back of the front wall

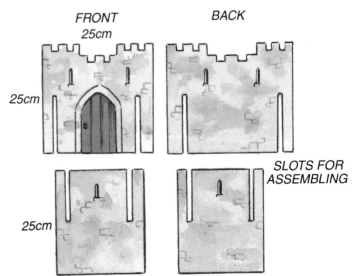

FRONT
25cm

BACK

25cm

SLOTS FOR
ASSEMBLING

25cm

20cm

of the castle with strong adhesive tape. This box must be filled with as many bits of 'treasure' as you can find. Of course, it doesn't have to be real gold. It's amazing how expensive a string of plastic beads looks after it has been sprayed with gold paint, and shiny metallic paper wrappings from candles can be turned into impressive fake bangles and rings. Brass chains look like gold, and take up very little space when packed.

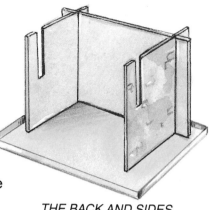

THE BACK AND SIDES ASSEMBLED ON TRAY

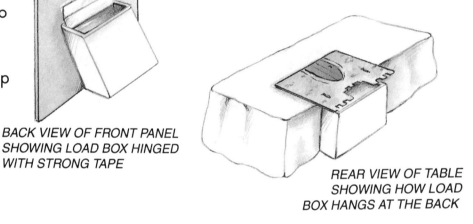

BACK VIEW OF FRONT PANEL SHOWING LOAD BOX HINGED WITH STRONG TAPE

SET UP

All the goodies are loaded into the secret box, and the front wall is placed flat on your table, with the load box hanging down behind it. The table-cloth covering the table will hide the load box from the view of the audience. The two sides and the back of the castle are laid on top of the front wall, and the tray is placed to one side of the table.

PERFORMANCE

First show the tray. Then pick up the back wall and two sides and assemble them on the tray in their correct positions, so that you can see inside the model castle. Pick up the front wall, bringing it straight up to a vertical position, so that the load box swings into position out of sight behind it. Insert the front wall into the slots in the side walls. This brings the load box into position inside the castle, and as it is now hidden by all four walls you can turn the tray around to show all sides of the castle.

Finish telling your story, then reach inside the castle and bring out the treasure.

REAR VIEW OF TABLE SHOWING HOW LOAD BOX HANGS AT THE BACK

SEEING WITH YOUR FINGERTIPS

Your friends will probably laugh when you tell them that your fingertips are so sensitive that they can detect the high value cards in a pack of playing cards. But you can bewilder them all by this wonderful demonstration of sleight-of-finger. Hand them a pack of cards to be thoroughly shuffled so that you could not possibly know the position of any of the cards. Take the pack back and hold it out of sight behind you. Now ask your friends what are the high value cards in a pack. Some will say aces, and some will say the kings. Ask them which they prefer – kings or aces.

Whatever they say, pretend that you are pleased, because – "Those are the easy ones!" Let us suppose that they choose the aces. You pretend to sort out the cards behind your back, and bring out all the four aces one by one. It is quite natural that your friends will now challenge you to find the kings, since you implied that they were more difficult. So, reluctantly, you start sorting again, pretending that it is mush harder this time, and therefore taking a little longer. Finally, you triumphantly bring out the four kings all together, which will be a surprise

and guarantee you plenty of applause.

Now you know the secret. You will have a lot of fun watching them feel the aces and kings to see if they can detect any difference from the other cards.

The secret

You will need a safety pin and a strong rubber band. Pin the band to the back of your trousers or skirt, just below the belt or

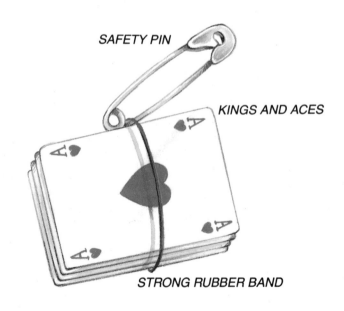

SAFETY PIN

KINGS AND ACES

STRONG RUBBER BAND

waistband. Take all the aces and kings out of the pack, and insert them into the rubber band, being sure to remember which way round they are. Then you will have to put on a jacket or loose sweater or tee shirt which is long enough to hide the cards.

Performance

Have the pack shuffled, and put it behind your back. While you are talking about which cards they want you to find, take the kings and aces out of the rubber band. As soon as you know which cards you are going to find first, add the eight cards to the pack with the appropriate cards on the outside, making them easy to get at. Bring them out one by one, but act as if you really are having to search through the whole pack. Bring the second lot of four cards out together, because that makes for a better climax.

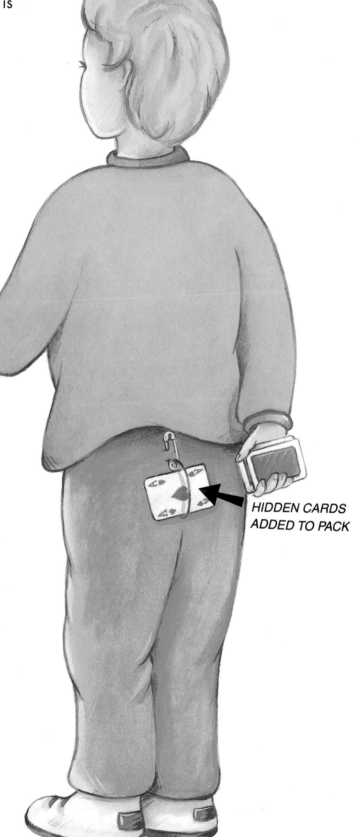

HIDDEN CARDS
ADDED TO PACK

THE MAGNETIC CUP

You will require two things that the audience can see for this trick, and one secret device that they must never know about.

Taking an ordinary stainless steel table knife, you hold it straight out in front of you with the blade in a flat position. Then you take a thin plastic or paper cup and balance it on the end of the blade. Carefully, you put your free hand on the top of the cup, and slowly turn the whole lot upside down. Then you take your hand away very dramatically, and wonder of wonders, the cup stays clinging to the knife, as if it was magically attracted in some way. You take hold of the cup again, then remove the knife and hand it out for examination, followed by the cup.

THE ALTERNATIVE

CLEAR PLASTIC GLASS

MAGNET INSIDE SILK HANDKERCHIEF

THE SECRET

Hidden in your hand at the start of the trick is a small powerful magnet. Before placing the cup on the knife, you let the magnet slide into the bottom of the cup. If you put a bit of stretchy first-aid plaster around the magnet, that will help to deaden any noise.

Naturally, when the cup is placed on the knife then turned upside down the magnet will hold it in place – that's what magnets do! At the end of the trick, when you put your free hand under the mouth of the inverted cup, you grasp it firmly then slide the knife off and hand it to a spectator. This allows the magnet to drop into the hand holding the cup. Now use your other hand to give the cup to an onlooker. This leaves the magnet in your hand to get rid of into a pocket as soon as everyone is looking at the cup and knife. The best type of cup to use is one that has the bottom level with the outside edge of the cup. You could even do this trick with a clear plastic tumbler – the disposable variety used for parties. Obviously the magnet would be visible, so you wrap it in a thin silk handkerchief, and tuck that into the glass, as if to make the trick look more attractive.

As a safer alternative to the knife you could use a metal ruler.

MAGNET COVERED IN STICKY PLASTER DROPPED SECRETLY INTO THE CUP

MAGNET SECRETLY DROPS INTO HAND WHEN KNIFE IS LIFTED

RINGS OFF

Although the title of this trick mentions rings, it can be done with door keys, metal washers, Chinese coins, or mints with a hole - in fact anything that has a small hole in it. Whatever is used you will need about half a dozen of them, plus a piece of string, wool, ribbon, or tape about 45cm long, together with a dark-coloured handkerchief.

What you do

Thread one of the rings on to the string, and tie the ends of the string together to form a loop. Now thread the remaining rings on to the loop. Obviously these rings will not fall off the loop because they are trapped by the first ring. Lay the loop on your left hand as shown in the picture, with the single ring hanging over the edge near your thumb, and the other five rings in your palm. Close your fingers over these five rings.

DARK-COLOURED HANDKERCHIEF

HAND CLOSED AND TURNED OVER BENEATH HANDKERCHIEF

PICK UP LOOP HERE

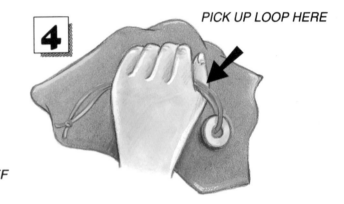

Now cover your fist with the handkerchief – at the same time secretly turning your fist over. Reach through the handkerchief with your right thumb and forefinger and grip one side of the string loop just above the single ring. Gently lift up the handkerchief. This will pull the loop free of the five rings, leaving them in your hand. Pretend to pull them free of the loop, and bring them out from under the handkerchief. Then uncover the loop to show the first ring is still in place.

If you use objects with small holes and a thick wool loop, you will be able to open your left hand and lift the loop up, but the rings will stay jammed on the loop until you pull them off one by one. You could even get someone to hold the loop through the handkerchief while you do this.

THE MAGIC SPELL

You don't need a whole pack for this trick, just a little packet of eleven cards. The packet is given to a spectator to shuffle well. Then you ask him to deal the cards face down into two piles of five cards. Naturally he will have one card left over, and since the cards were shuffled you can have no idea of what that card is. Ask the spectator to remember the name of the card, then put it on top of either pile then put the other pile on top of that.

You now pick up the complete packet of cards and ask what is the name of the remembered card. Let us suppose it is the 'Ten of Hearts'. You spell out the name of the card – T-E-N-O-F-H-E-A-R-T-S – by dealing the first card onto the table saying 'T', then putting the second card on the bottom of the packet. The third card goes onto the table saying 'E', and the next to the bottom of the packet. The fifth card spell 'N', and so on, spelling letters and putting alternate cards on the bottom of the packet until you arrive at the letter 'S', when you will have only one card left in your hand, and that will be the 'Ten of Hearts'.

DEAL ONE, PUT ONE UNDER

The Secret

The eleven cards comprise the following: the Ace, 2, 6, and 10 of Hearts, the 4, 5, 9, and the Jack of Clubs, and the 2, 6, and 10 of Spades. The simple secret is that the names of these cards are spelt with eleven letters. If you follow the instruction carefully the spectator's card finishes up the sixth card down in the assembled packet. By alternately spelling a letter and putting one under the packet this will automatically make the correct card the last one to be dealt.

One little word of warning. Be careful to deal letters only when you are dealing cards on the table. There is a temptation to spell letters as you put the cards on the bottom of the packet, but that would ruin the trick.

THE BANGL

A bangle is not the only thing you could use for this trick. There are several other objects that could be employed, such as a finger ring, an embroidery hoop, a large key, or even a wire coat hanger. All that is necessary is that the item forms a complete circle without any gaps. The best plan is to try and borrow something suitable – which makes the trick seem more impressive. The other props you will require are a piece of string or soft cord about 150cm long, and a large head-square or small table-cloth.

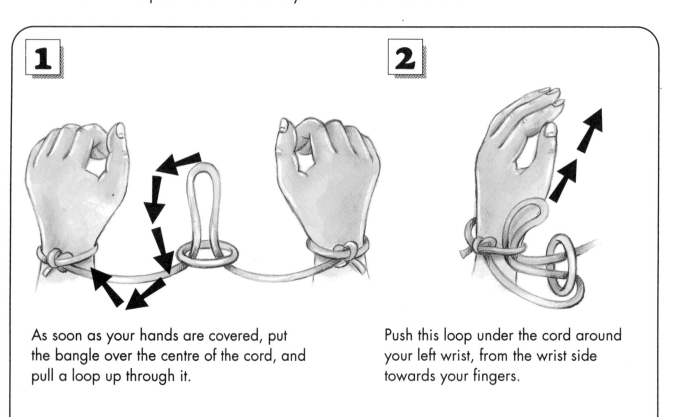

1 As soon as your hands are covered, put the bangle over the centre of the cord, and pull a loop up through it.

2 Push this loop under the cord around your left wrist, from the wrist side towards your fingers.

The action

You request someone to tie each end of the cord securely to your wrists, using lots of knots, then give you the bangle in one hand. Now you have both hands covered with the cloth. After a few moments you allow the cloth to fall away, and your audience is surprised to see that the bangle has not only been passed onto the cord, but has been knotted into place. Since you could not possibly untie and re-tie the cord round your wrists, this feat seems quite impossible.

The secret

You will understand this more easily if you look at the illustrations very carefully, and follow the instructions step by step.

3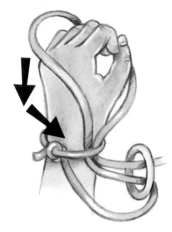

Pull the loop right up and over the hand.

4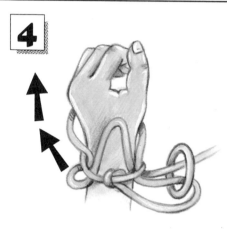

Push the loop down through the cord around the outside of the wrist.

5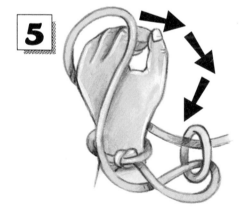

Pull the loop back over the hand again.

It may seem a little complicated at first, but if you try it out a few times, you will find that you can do it very quickly.

An old version of this trick used a duplicate bangle hidden up your sleeve, but this method is more baffling since the bangle may be borrowed.

6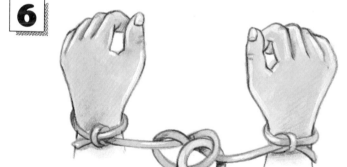

Slide the bangle to the middle of the cord with the knot around it, then pull on the cord to tighten the knot.

7 Uncover your hands, and take a bow.

BLACK MAGIC

This is a clever mind-reading stunt which is ideal for performing at a party. You leave the room while everyone gathers around to choose an object that they can see in the room – just like the game of 'I spy'. When you return to the room you successfully identify the object. For this one you need a secret partner, who seems to be just a member of the audience asked to help, but is really the most important part of the trick. When you arrive back in the room he points to many different objects in the room, without saying a word or giving any indication by the way he points. You shake your head each time and say "No, that's not the one." Finally your secret confederate touches the chosen object and you say "Yes, that's it!"

NO!

NO

The secret

Every time your partner touches an object it can be any colour except black, but the object that he touches just before the chosen must be black. So as soon as he touches a black object you know that the chosen object will be next.

NO!

NO

NO

THAT'S THE ONE!

You can repeat this a few times, and it will seem more and more baffling, especially if your confederate points to a different black object every time. If there are not many black items in the room use white instead.

THE

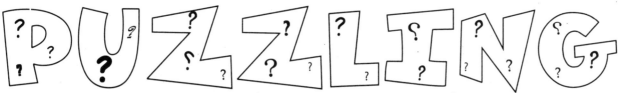

Carefully copy the drawing of the old man with a beard on to a piece of paper measuring about 20cm by 10cm. Ask your friends if they can think why he looks so unhappy. Maybe it's because he has only one hair left on his head.

Let's try a little magic to cheer him up.

1

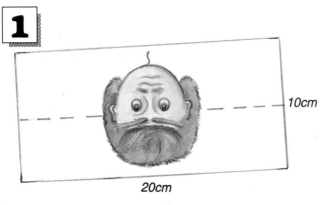

10cm

20cm

Hold the paper in both hands with the picture facing you. Turn a little sideways so that your friends can see it too.

2

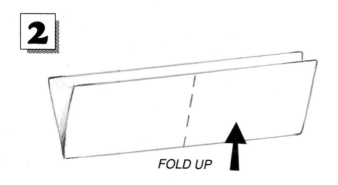

FOLD UP

Fold the bottom edge up to the top along the dotted line.

3

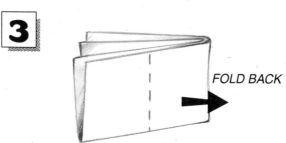

FOLD BACK

Now fold the right side away from you so that it goes behind the left half.

4

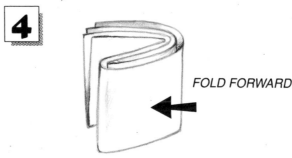

FOLD FORWARD

Then fold the right side towards you in front of the left side.

Now – without turning it or twisting it in any way, unfold the paper as if you were turning the pages of a book.

If you have followed the instructions carefully the face will have changed to a portrait of the old man when he was young, with lots of hair. Of course it's really the same face upside down – but how did it happen? Practise the folding so that you can do it smoothly and quickly. Emphasise the fact that at no time do you turn the paper upside down. Try making up your own picture that changes like this.

THE INCREDIBLE SHRINKING PENCIL

Sometimes it is quite a good idea to pretend a certain thing is going to happen, but really do something quite different, so that your audience is taken completely by surprise. This is a good trick to do while you are sitting at the dining table.

What happens

Pointing to a pencil in front of you on the table, you announce that you are going to perform the incredible vanishing pencil trick. Lifting it up in front of your eyes, you gaze at it for a moment or two. Nothing happens, so you put the pencil back where it was, blow on your hands, blow on the pencil, then pick it up again. But now you push your hands together as if trying to squeeze the pencil out of existence. Suddenly you seem to give up, as if the trick is not going to work, and open your hands. Surprise, surprise, the pencil has not vanished, but merely shrunk to a third of its original size.

The secret

You will not be surprised to learn that you require a short piece of pencil as well as the original long pencil, and of course they must match as to colour and shape. The short piece should measure about 5cm, and at the start it is concealed in your left hand between the second joint of your second finger and the middle of your palm.

Performance

With your right hand place the long pencil about 10cm away from the edge of the table, and draw your audience's attention to it, saying that you will make it disappear. Grasp the pencil with both hands, fingers on top and thumbs underneath so that it is completely covered. Now slide it towards yourself until it reaches the edge of the table, then lift it up in front of your eyes, pretending to concentrate really hard.

When nothing happens, put the pencil back where it was on the table. Blow on your hands and the pencil, pretending that will

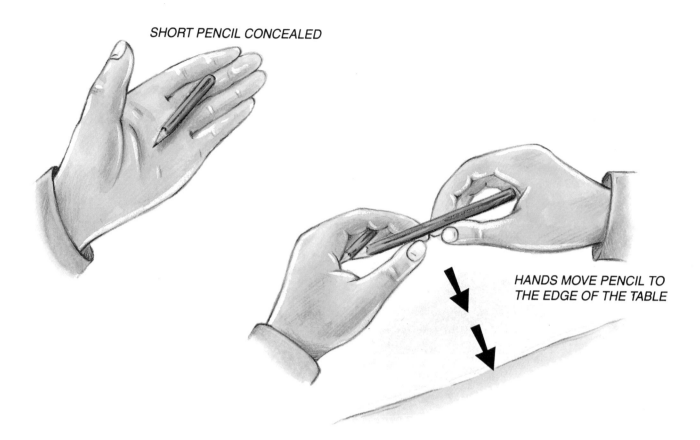

SHORT PENCIL CONCEALED

HANDS MOVE PENCIL TO
THE EDGE OF THE TABLE

help to make the trick work, then grasp the pencil exactly as before, and slide it towards yourself. However, this time, when your hands reach the edge of the table, you let the long pencil drop into your lap. Continuing as if you are still holding the pencil, lift your hands up in front of your eyes, push them together, then open them to reveal the short pencil which has been hidden in the left hand all the time.

Forget about the pencil on your lap until you have a chance to get rid of it when no-one is looking.

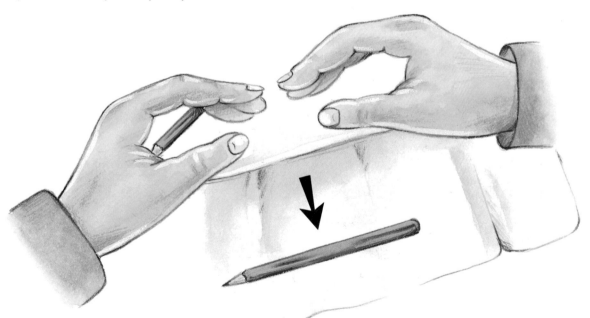

LONG PENCIL FALLS
INTO YOUR LAP

Wizardry with Wool

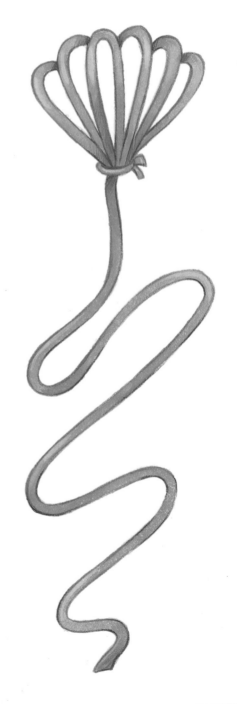

Magicians have always been fond of cutting things up and then putting them back together. In fact the famous 'Cut and Restored Rope Trick' is described in one of the very first books of magic -'Discoveries of Witchcraft' by Reginald Scot, published in 1584. It seems a bit daft really, because if you didn't cut the rope in the first place you wouldn't need to restore it, but as long as it baffles and entertains an audience magicians will keep on doing it.

Here's a version of the trick which uses wool, instead of rope. You need to find some really thick wool, like that used for making rugs, and it should be as bright a colour as possible.

Preparation

Cut off a two-metre length of wool. Then pleat one end of it into six little loops as shown in picture. These should take up about a quarter of the wool. Tie a short piece of wool around the bottom of the loops to keep them together.

Performance

Hide the bundle of loops in your left hand, and hold the other end of the wool in your right hand. Stretch the wool out between your hands to display it. Now start gathering the wool into large loops, starting about 30cm from the left hand and placing the top of each loop into the left fingers. This should result in six large loops hanging from the left hand. Now with your right hand reach into the top of the left hand and pull out the ends of the small loops. It should look as if they are really the tops of the large loops.

Pick up your scissors and snip through the little loops one by one, letting your audience see that they are really being cut. Then trim the ends to make them even, the little pieces falling on the floor acting as convincing proof that the wool has been cut into several pieces.

Pretend to pick up a tube of 'invisible glue', and squirt it over the ends of the wool. Then push the ends down into your fist, and keep tight hold of what's left of the bundle of little loops while you release the large loops to show that the wool has been magically 'glued' back into one whole length. Tug on the wool to show it really is restored, then gather it up, put it away in your box of tricks, and carry on with your next illusion.

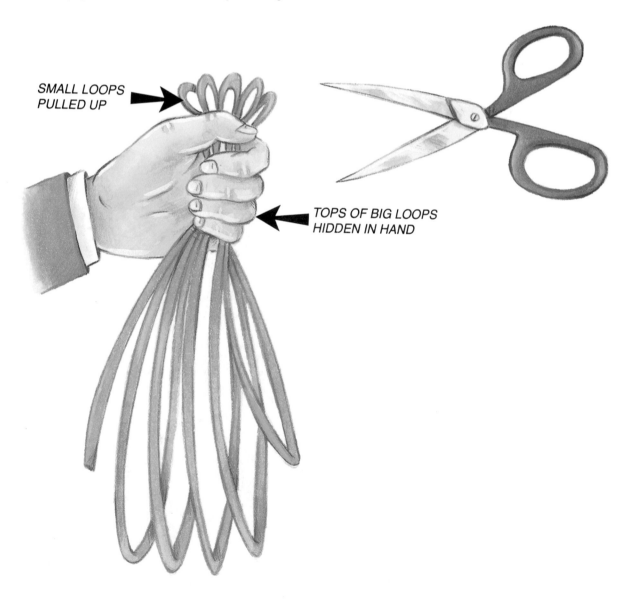

SMALL LOOPS
PULLED UP

TOPS OF BIG LOOPS
HIDDEN IN HAND

CONFETTI CONFECTION

Your audience is going to like this, because the end result is most enjoyable. You show a cardboard box which is half full of confetti, then you take a colourful canister and dip it into the box to fill it with confetti. You pour the confetti back into the box from a little way above it so that everyone can see clearly what it is. After repeating this action a couple of times you bring up the filled canister for the last time, then level off any surplus confetti from the top of the can, and wrap it in a sheet of tissue paper.

Once the can is wrapped you take up your magic wand, wave it over the parcel and say the magic words - "FROGS, TOADS, RATS AND MICE, CHANGE CONFETTI TO SOMETHING NICE". Then you puncture the tissue paper covering the top of the can, and pour out a quantity of brightly wrapped candies, which you offer round to your audience. I told you they would enjoy this trick!

REQUIREMENTS

You need a cardboard box about 30cm by 20cm by 20cm deep. This should be decorated so that it looks special, then half filled with confetti. Next you require two tin cans, the sort that tinned soup comes in. They must be exactly the same size, and you

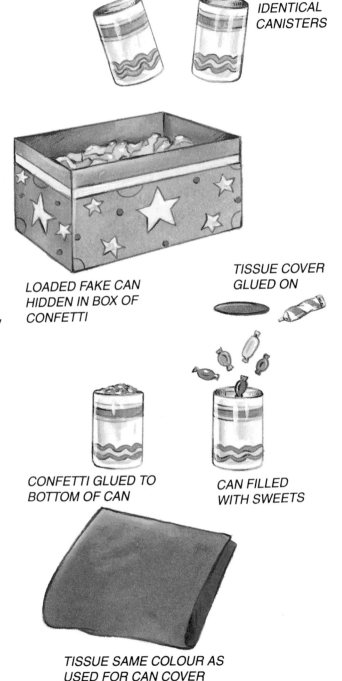

IDENTICAL CANISTERS

LOADED FAKE CAN HIDDEN IN BOX OF CONFETTI

TISSUE COVER GLUED ON

CONFETTI GLUED TO BOTTOM OF CAN

CAN FILLED WITH SWEETS

TISSUE SAME COLOUR AS USED FOR CAN COVER

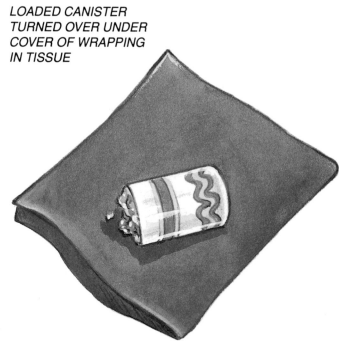

*LOADED CANISTER
TURNED OVER UNDER
COVER OF WRAPPING
IN TISSUE*

should get a grown-up to make sure there are no sharp edges where the can has been opened. Alternatively there are some kitchen products that come in cardboard canisters, which will work just as well. Both canisters should be decorated to look exactly alike.

*BURST TISSUE TO
PRODUCE SWEETS*

Now take one of the canisters, turn it upside down, and glue pieces of confetti all over the bottom. This is the can that will contain the load of sweets. There should be enough sweets to fill the can to the brim. Then glue a circle of tissue paper to the rim of the can to keep the sweets in place. Hide the loaded can in the box under the confetti. Have a double sheet of dark coloured tissue paper, a plate, your magic wand, and the unprepared can ready on your table, and you are all set to perform.

PERFORMANCE

Show the unprepared can to be perfectly empty, dip it into the box to scoop it full of confetti, lift it out, then let the confetti pour back into the box. Do this a couple of times. The third time you leave the ordinary can behind and bring out the loaded can. Obviously this must be held so that the end with the confetti stuck on is at the top, and you should try to get some loose confetti on top of it, which you can then brush off as if it is too full. Hold the loaded can with some fingers underneath the bottom so there is no chance of the tissue cover bursting too soon.

Now you pick up the double sheet of tissue and hold it in front of the can as you prepare to wrap it. This gives you enough cover to turn the can secretly up the other way so that the tissue-covered end is now at the top. Finish the wrapping, wave the wand, and say the words. Then use the wand to burst through the wrapping and the tissue cover, and pour the sweets out onto the plate. The confetti has changed to confectionery – much to your friends' delight. Drop the wrapped can back into the box out of sight.

A PAPER DAISY CHAIN

Quite often, when you see a magic show, the magician will include items which are not strictly magic, such as ventriloquism, puppets, or making animals from balloons. They are known as 'Allied Arts' and help to give a little variety to the performance. Here is a spot of paper-tearing which is always popular.

Preparation

1

FOLD SQUARE INTO FOUR QUARTERS

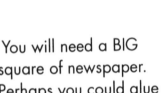

2

FOLD ALONG DOTTED LINE

3

You will need a BIG square of newspaper. Perhaps you could glue two sheets together, then cut out the largest square possible. Fold the square in half, then into quarters. Then fold it twice more as shown in the illustration. With a coloured crayon copy the design on to one side of the folded paper.

4

TEAR AWAY SHADED BITS

Performance

Unfold the newspaper to show that it is quite ordinary, but be sure to keep the design side away from the audience. Re-fold the paper exactly as it was, and carefully tear away the portions that are shaded in the diagram. Then shake the paper open gently to see the result.

Newspaper is usually used for this stunt because it is fairly easy to tear. If you use plain white or fancy coloured wrapping paper, you may need to use scissors to cut out the design, because the paper is thicker. Always be careful when handling scissors.

Why not try working out your own designs.

CLIPPING THE JACK

This is the sort of trick that you can carry around in your pocket and have a lot of fun with. It's a challenge which looks so easy, but you will even fool yourself when you try it out. It will only take a few minutes to make it up.

WHAT YOU NEED

Five playing cards. Four of these should be high value black spot cards, such as the Ten of Clubs or the Nine of Spades. The other card must be a Jack of Hearts or Diamonds. Arrange the cards in a row as shown in the picture, with the edges spaced about 15mm apart, and with the Jack in the centre, then glue them together. The only other item you need is a large paper-clip or bobby pin.

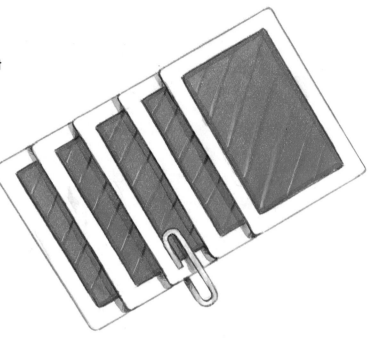

CARDS SPACED 15mm APART

PERFORMANCE

Show the block of cards to your friends, and ask them to note where the Jack is. Turn the cards face down, give them the paper-clip and ask them to clip it onto the Jack. Now turn the cards over again, and they will be amazed to find that the clip is nowhere near the Jack. Try it for yourself. It's really a sort of optical illusion that fools your eyes and senses.

One word of warning. Don't let too many people have a go at the same time, otherwise someone is bound to work out the secret.

THE MAGICIAN ESCAPES

One of the other tricks I have described in this book is called HOUDINI ESCAPES, in which a paper cut-out is released from a piece of string. Now we are going to do a similar escape, but this time with a full-size person.

The magician displays a length of string or narrow ribbon. It is about 10 metres long. He folds it into a loop, and pushes the loop through a buttonhole, passes the ends through the loop and pulls them tight. This makes a knot which would seem impossible to undo without passing the ends back through the loop. A member of the audience is asked to hold the loose ends of the ribbon while the magician goes outside the room and closes the door. He starts a count-down - very loudly so that everyone can hear it through the door. "TEN, NINE, EIGHT, SEVEN, SIX, ...", but before he gets to ZERO he opens the door and bursts back into the room completely free of the ribbon loop.

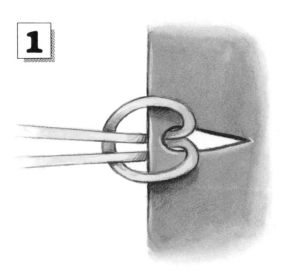

RIBBON LOOPED THROUGH BUTTONHOLE

The secret

As soon as he is outside the door, the magician loosens the knot and pulls on the loop until it is big enough to step through. Then the loop is lifted up and over his head as shown in the diagram. By doing this the ribbon will be freed from the button-hole.

When you try this feat of escapology, practise until you can do it very quickly, then your audience will be really astounded.

To make the stunt much more baffling, you can pass the ends of the ribbon through the keyhole before you leave the room. You may need a large bodkin or a bit of twisted wire to help you do this. Then when you are free of the loop you shout - "Pull the ribbon!" before you open the door. The ribbon loop will come through the keyhole without you – which is even more surprising.

2 LOOSEN THE LOOP

3 STEP THROUGH THE LOOP

4 PASS IT OVER THE HEAD

TORN TISSUE TO

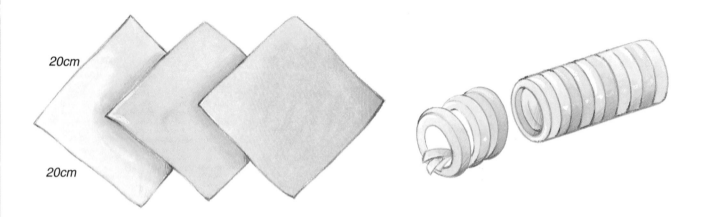

20cm

20cm

Some magic tricks are best performed with a spoken presentation, but there are many which work well in a silent act, accompanied by music. This is a very pretty trick that fits into the 'silent' category.

WHAT HAPPENS

The magician shows several pieces of brightly coloured tissue paper, which are torn into pieces then crushed into a ball. A sprinkling of 'magic salt' or a wave of the wand, then the wizard pulls out from his hand metres of coloured streamers.

WHAT YOU NEED

Go to a carnival or a party shop and buy a packet of streamers. Most of them come in a multicolored packet, which is just what you want. Pick out three individual streamers of contrasting colours, then get some tissue paper to match those colours.

Cut the tissue into squares about 20cm by 20cm. Put the three streamers together, pull out the middle ends of each one a little way and join them together and place them close to a corner on one of the squares of tissue. Now cut another piece of tissue about 10cm by 10cm, put glue just around the edge, and stick it over the streamers, like a patch or pocket. Try not to get any glue on the streamers themselves. For your performance you will need this prepared tissue plus two unprepared sheets of the appropriate colours. The prepared sheet should be placed on your table with the pocket side down, and the other sheets on top.

PERFORMANCE

Pick up the three sheets of tissue, keeping the pocket side towards yourself. Hold them with the pocket corner held under your thumb. Pull out the unprepared sheets with your other hand and wave them about a

STREAMERS

INNER ENDS
TAPED TOGETHER

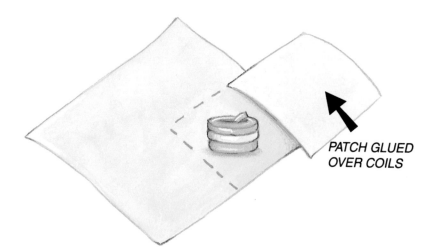

PATCH GLUED
OVER COILS

bit. Put them back together with the prepared sheet, and tear them all in half, then in half again. Now crush all the pieces together into your left hand. At the same time you must manage to break open the pocket and find the taped ends of the streamers. Start pulling the streamers out with plenty of excitement. When they come to an end, quickly crush up the remaining tissue paper into a very small

bundle, and hide it by scooping up the streamers with both hands. Hold the bunch of streamers up in the air, and take a bow.

ALL THAT GLITTERS IS NOT GOLD

When a trick is fairly easy and quick to perform, it sometimes needs to be dressed up with a story. This holds your audience, and they listen to you as much as they watch the trick

This is one of those tricks - and here is the story you tell to entertain your audience.

There once was a King and his only son and they lived in a great castle. One day the prince went to the King. "Father", he said, "I am grown now and it is time I went out into the world to seek my fortune. Please may I do this?" The King was sad to hear his son's request, but he knew he could not deny his son the opportunity to discover the world for himself. "You have my permission," he told his son. "You may take one of two precious gifts with you. One is a large juicy apple and the other is a block of gold."

The prince considered carefully, and chose the gold as he thought it would be the most valuable for his journey.

The prince travelled for many days until he reached a dry desert region, where no people lived. He carried on, growing hungrier and thirstier. At last he stopped. The block of gold seemed to be weighing him down. He decided to throw the gold away - it was no good to him. But first he opened the box, and found instead that the gold had changed into an apple! A few bites and his thirst was quenched and he carried on his journey, out of the desert.
And where was the block of gold? That was safely in the King's treasure room, back in the castle.

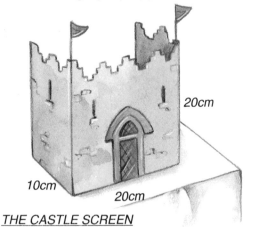

20cm

10cm

20cm

THE CASTLE SCREEN

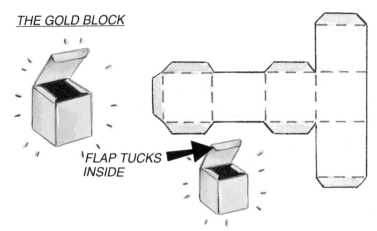

THE GOLD BLOCK

'FLAP TUCKS INSIDE'

PREPARATION:

To perform the trick you need a screen, painted and cut out to represent the castle, an apple (plastic or wax if you can get one) and the block of gold made from cardboard and painted gold.

You also need a 'shell' block of gold, made in the same way as the gold block but with one side missing. The inside of the 'shell' must be painted black. Also the apple must fit in this. Then you make a jewelled casket into which the shell will fit snugly. It should

have a separate lid and paint the inside of this box black as well. Then stand the castle on the table with the apple and gold block directly behind it. Stand the gold 'shell' on top of the block, open side up. Place the jewelled casket and lid beside the castle, on view.

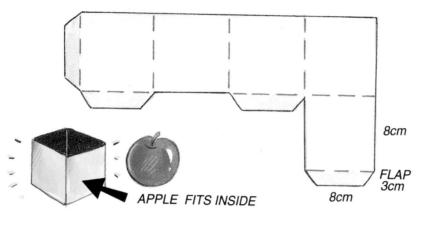

APPLE FITS INSIDE

SET-UP

8cm

FLAP
3cm

8cm

GOLD BLOCK

PERFORMANCE:

Now tell the story of the King and his son, in your own words.

When you reach the part where the prince must choose between the block of gold and the apple, lift the castle screen revealing the gold block and apple, but holding onto the 'shell' with your thumb so that it is lifted with the castle. Put the screen back on the table, directly behind the gold block and the apple. Let the 'shell' drop to the table behind the screen.

Have a soft cloth on the table to deaden the sound.

Show your audience the gold and the apple, continuing with the story, and then put them back behind the castle.

Put the apple straight into the 'shell' and the gold block beside the 'shell', on the table. Now pick up the jewelled casket, and show it empty to your audience. Reach behind the screen for the gold 'shell', and put the 'shell' inside the jewelled casket, keeping it tipped slightly towards you, and then put on the lid.

Continue telling the story, remembering that the casket should be becoming heavier and heavier.

When you reach the point where the prince opens the box, remove the lid of the casket, and gently squeezing the sides to keep the shell in place, tip

the casket up to drop the apple out. You can even show the audience the empty casket. Then remove the castle screen to reveal the gold back where it should be.

Finally fold the screen flat to end the trick, showing that nothing could possible have been behind it.

BLACK INSIDE

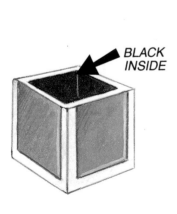

LID

JEWEL BOX

THE DISAPPEARING POM POM

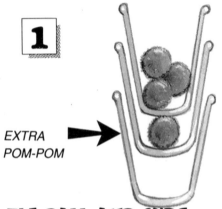

1

EXTRA
POM-POM

THE BALL AND CUPS

This trick, using cups and balls, is probably one of the world's oldest, and was even performed in Ancient Rome! It is still popular with magicians and audiences today.
Being such an old trick there are many ways of doing it, but if you follow these simple step-by-step instructions, you will soon be entertaining your friends with ease.

2

PREPARATION:

All you need are three plastic or paper cups (they need to stack together), four small woolly pompoms, and, of course, your magic wand. Stack the cups, with the three woolly pompoms in the top cup, and the fourth pompom hidden in the middle cup.

PERFORMANCE:

Now, to perform the trick, have the three cups in your left hand, and tip the three pompoms from the top cup onto the table. Hold the stacked cups upright and take the bottom cup in your right hand. Your right thumb must be on the far side of the cup, and your fingers curled up underneath to be pointing towards you. This positioning is very important.

Now, with the right hand in this position pull the bottom cup down, holding the top two with your left hand. Turn the cup down, to end up upside down on the left hand side of the table. Make this downward move as smoothly as possible, as this is the basic move upon which the trick is

3

based. Practise until you can do it easily.

Repeat this move with the second cup, ensuring thumb and fingers are correctly positioned, and place the second cup in the centre of the table. This is the cup holding the fourth, and hidden, pompom. If you do the cup move smoothly and at the right speed, the hidden pompom will not fall out, and by turning the

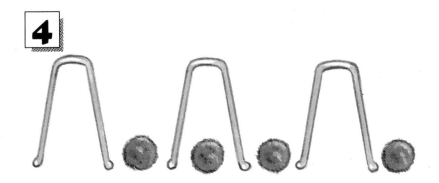

4

cup toward you, the pompom will not be seen by your audience.

Turn the third cup upside down in the same way and place it on the right hand side of the table. Arrange the three pompoms in front of the cups. Tell your audience to watch carefully.

Take one pompom and place it on the middle cup. Take the other cups one at a time and cover the centre cup, and the pompom. Tap the cups with your magic wand, and lift up all three cups together.

middle cup again.

Do the basic move again, but this time put the middle cup over the pompom on the table, so that you know there are now two pompoms beneath the cup and the other two pompoms can be seen on the table.

Put one of these pompoms on the centre cup, and cover again with the other two cups. Now tap twice with your magic wand. Lift the stack of cups to reveal the two balls on the table. Again, you have a pompom hidden in the middle cup.

pompoms beneath the cups. Pause for some applause from your audience - this is the first trick completed.

Now for something slightly different - with the three cups in your left hand, using the basic move, put the first cup down on the left, the middle cup, with the hidden pompom, on the right and the last in the centre. Don't cover any pompoms this time.

Tell your audience you will do something different this time. Take one pompom and put it on the left hand cup and then cover with the middle cup. Tell your audience you will now send the pompom through the cup, across the table, and then make it appear under the right hand cup. Tap the cups twice with your magic wand.

Lift the two cups together to show the bottom one is empty and then lift the right hand cup

5

 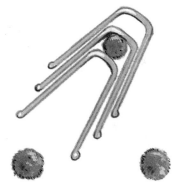

6

Magically the pompom seems to have gone through the bottom cup to the table, as your audience sees the 'fourth' pompom revealed for the first time. You now have three stacked cups on your left hand, with one pompom hidden in the

With the cups in your left hand, repeat the basic move, this time covering the two pompoms with the middle cup. Once again, cover the centre cup with the other cups. Three taps of your magic wand and this time there are three

to show the pompom has arrived - take a bow!

To finish, stack the two cups inside the third, which will keep the hidden pompom out of sight and put the three pompoms inside the next cup. Now put the whole trick away.